If you're heading off into the wonderfu[barcode] book to take with you. And if you've be pick it up for the rest of your journey. T work is the key message, and most impor. that God is interested in all the work we do. It's easy to read, practical, and encourages the reader to bring glory to God at work. Personal stories and challenging questions bring alive our understanding of the Bible and its relationship to life at work – such as, 'Can you name one thing that you have changed in your life in the last month as a result of what you've read in the Bible? Just one thing.' There are no platitudes in this book; just straight-talking encouragement to be who God created us to be. Chickens, yucca plants, hedgehogs and weirdos all feature along the way – you can decide where you fit in, or do you want to travel against the flow?
Daphne Clifton, Business Coach

This book is a breath of fresh air that explains with wit and wisdom what it means to 'think Christianly' about the world of work. If you are just starting or well established in your job, here is a readable and practical guide that will even help you survive with David Brent as your boss.
Ian Coffey, Director of Leadership Training, Moorlands College

Have you ever said to yourself, 'if I was starting again, I would not start from here'? Jago has written with sharp insights and practical pointers to help us avoid such remorse as we begin our working lives. It is biblical, upbeat, and wide-ranging, and includes references to sex, money and stress – a potentially wilting trinity in any workplace. Well-chosen case studies and examples provide a solid foundation for the ups and downs of working life, which begins here and carries through into the whole of eternity. A good investment for a massive return.
Rodney Green, former Chief Executive, Leicester City Council

Outstanding, realistic, challenging and a really good read. Jago Wynne writes with a light touch, but with considerable depth. He handles the Bible with admirable coherence, and deeply understands the tears, challenges and joys of life at work. This is hardly surprising for someone who has helped many thousands connect their faith to their working lives in what many have valued as his quite exceptional ministry in London's West End. Now more than ever our places of work need the kind of transformation this book so effectively portrays. If you want to find out what it means to walk more closely with God and be a working disciple of Jesus Christ, this is definitely for you.

Michael Lawson, Archdeacon of Hampstead, and Chairman of the Church of England Evangelical Council

Connecting our faith with our work is a constant struggle for many of us. Is God interested in my work? How do I serve God Monday to Friday, 9–5? These are questions I hear a lot and Working Without Wilting gives answers that are well grounded in the reality of the workplace and the truths from God's word. Whether you're just starting out in the workplace or you've been working for a large percentage of your life, this book will help you understand your role as a Christian worker and give you practical applications to take straight into work with you on Monday morning.

Charmaine Muir, Workplace Ministry Worker, All Souls, Langham Place

Jago Wynne has written a comprehensive handbook in terms of helping individual Christians and churches think through what it means to live for Christ in the world at work. There is wisdom and insight on page after page and frankly I'd like to make it compulsory reading for anyone beginning their working life.

Rico Tice, Associate Minister, All Souls, Langham Place and co-author of Christianity Explored

This is a must-read for those starting work! It will make you laugh out loud as well as challenge you in wanting to live for God at work. The pages are littered with real-life experiences and biblical truth to provide wisdom in dealing with the practical situations you may face at work. Jago's passion to see the Christian not only survive, but thrive in their workplace is infectious. Are you up for the adventure of worshipping God at work, being the trout that swims up stream and seeing God work through you to impact those around you? What a privilege – Bring it on!

Ros Turner, Groups Support Manager, TransformWorkUK

Full of practical advice with plenty of amusement thrown in – Jago Wynne's empathetic and active approach to living the Christian life at work is refreshing. I like the creative way in which he relates real-life experience of the workplace to the wisdom in the text. Especially for Christians in the early years of working, Working Without Wilting is a reality check and a great roadmap.

Paul Valler, former Finance & Human Resources Director, Hewlett-Packard Ltd

Jago Wynne

WORKING
without
WILTING

Starting well to finish strong

ivp

Inter-Varsity Press
Norton Street, Nottingham NG7 3HR, England
Email: ivp@ivpbooks.com
Website: www.ivpbooks.com

First published 2009
Reprinted 2010

British Library Cataloguing in Publication Data
A catalogue record for this book is available from the British Library.

ISBN 978-1-84474-372-8

Set in Dante 12/15
Typeset in Great Britain by CRB Associates, Potterhanworth, Lincolnshire
Printed and bound in Great Britain by Ashford Colour Press Ltd, Gosport,
Hampshire

Inter-Varsity Press publishes Christian books that are true to the Bible and that
communicate the gospel, develop discipleship and strengthen the church for its
mission in the world.

Inter-Varsity Press is closely linked with the Universities and Colleges Christian
Fellowship, a student movement connecting Christian Unions in universities
and colleges throughout Great Britain, and a member movement of the
International Fellowship of Evangelical Students. Website: *www.uccf.org.uk*

For Susannah –
who gave me my yucca plant

CONTENTS

PART4: WORK LIKE A TRUMPET

Flourishing for God in the workplace

SERIES PREFACE

A time for courage
Work matters hugely.

Work is the primary activity God created us to pursue – in communion with him and in partnership with others. Indeed, one of work's main goals is to make God's world a better place for all God's creatures to flourish in – to his glory.

Yes, work matters hugely.

And to many people it brings the joys of purpose shared, relationships deepened, talents honed, character shaped, obstacles overcome, products made, people served and money earned – even amid the inevitable frustrations, failures and disagreements of working life in even the best of organizations.

Yes, work matters hugely. And the financial crisis that began in 2008 only served to reinforce that reality as many found themselves without paid employment, many more with less money and many, many more were gripped by the fear of losing their jobs. However, long before the crisis, work had been getting harder, longer, less satisfying and more draining. Work had stretched its voracious tentacles into almost every area of life, sucking out the zing and whoosh and ease from time with family, friends, hobbies and community activities. UK citizens, for example, work four hours longer per person per week than the citizens of any other EU nation. We live in Slave New World.

How do we follow Jesus faithfully and fruitfully in such conditions?

Is coping – getting through the week – the height of our ambition? Surely not. But do we have good news for the workplace? Not just a truth to proclaim but a way to follow.

Not just a way to follow but life, divine life, to infuse the quality of our work, the quality of our relationships at work, and the quality of our contribution to the culture of the organizations in which we work? In our current context, we need not only biblical insight and divine empowerment, but also courage to make tough decisions about work and life, and courage to make tough decisions at work. Furthermore, at this time of national soul-searching about our economy and the values that drive it, we need to learn not only how to be faithful servants in the work culture we find ourselves in, but also to become proactive, positive shapers of that culture.

That's what the Faith at Work series is designed to do: take on the tough issues facing workers and offer material that's fresh, either because it brings new insights to familiar topics or because the author's particular background and experience open up enlightening vistas. We've also tried to write the books so that there's something nutritious and tasty, not only for the leisurely diner, but also for the snacker snatching a quick read on a train, or in a break, or, indeed, at the end of a demanding day.

The Lord be with you as you read. And the Lord be with you as you seek to follow him faithfully and courageously in your workplace.

Mark Greene
Series Editor
London Institute for Contemporary Christianity
2009

Volumes include:
Get a Life Paul Valler
Working it Out Ian Coffey
Working Models for our Time Mark Greene (commissioned)

ACKNOWLEDGMENTS

A big thank you to the congregations of All Souls Midweek and St Paul's Midweek, the members of the Breakfast Bible Study and the whole All Souls, Langham Place church family. Thank you for your patience with me, your love for applying God's Word into your work, and your willingness to be honest with me about the challenges you face in living for Christ at work. Thank you especially to the many people whom I quizzed in preparation for this book.

Thank you to Charmaine Muir, Lizzie Waterworth, Tim Dulley, Andy Stewart, Andrew Brown, Alice Hutchison, Mark Greene, two anonymous individuals and my mum for really pertinent comments on the first draft of the manuscript.

Thanks to Kate Byrom at IVP for suggesting writing this book at just the right time – and for her invaluable help throughout the whole process.

Thanks to the three people who have mentored me at various points over the last decade – Bill Wilson, Paul Williams and Michael Lawson. I have learnt far more about Christ-likeness from each of you than you realize.

Thanks to Daisy and Boaz for putting up with a dad who was in his office at times when they wanted him to be out of it.

And above all thanks to my wife, Susannah for her comments on the script, her encouragement in the whole process, and her love for the author.

Many true stories have been used in this book, but some names and some details have been changed to protect the identity of the individuals involved.

FOREWORD

When I met Jago through his growing workplace ministry at All Souls in London, it was clear that he was a man with a mission. It was quite obvious that he was passionate about encouraging people, especially young people, to live a seamless Christian life at work that does not divide up their Christian experience into a sacred and secular dead end.

This primer for the workplace will be especially sought after by those starting out in their working careers and also by those who have been seasoned in the workplace, but for whom the idea that God has an interest in their work is a foreign one.

Throughout the book one can see the disciplined approach of a management consultant. He knows how to pull together ideas that belong and at the same time to separate out rigorously the false and the misleading. We can imagine him, if he had remained in consultancy, armed with a PowerPoint presentation, coaxing mandates from his clients! He has retained this facility for persuasion and drawing material together through lucid writing and arresting headings. Well-argued and illustrated points draw out the stated and implicit message on every page of the book. Work and worship grow intimately together.

At a time like this, when we are undergoing what the *Financial Times* calls a 'mammoth shock' to the economy, we need to ask urgently as the writer to the Hebrews did, 'What is unshakeable in our lives? What will survive this great shaking?' The book helps us to find true security in a living daily relationship with Christ in the workplace, recognizing all the while the reality of the stresses at work.

One often hears that it is those at work who are in the front line in advancing the kingdom. In this view the clergy merely play a supportive role. But we should not allow this view to diminish the distinctive contribution of a pastor (for that is what Jago really is), mapping out a biblical view that will enable our daily lives to flourish as we see our work as part of our worship.

Ken Costa
Chairman of Lazard International Bank, Chairman of Alpha International and author of *God at Work*

INTRODUCTION: WORKING WITHOUT WILTING

Don't laugh, but I did geography at university. It meant I was qualified for colouring in maps with my crayons – but not much else. It also meant that, after university, I had to look for a job that didn't require any qualifications beyond the ability of me and my crayons. Management consultancy seemed the perfect fit.

You may have heard of the shepherd who was tending his flock in a remote pasture when suddenly a dust cloud approached at high speed, out of which emerged a shiny silver BMW. The driver, a young man in an Armani suit, poked his head out of the window and addressed the shepherd. 'Hey! If I can tell you how many sheep you have in your flock, will you give me one?'

The shepherd looked at the man, then glanced at his peacefully grazing flock and answered, 'Sure.'

The driver parked his car, plugged his mobile into his laptop and surfed the web to a GPS satellite imaging system to initiate a remote body-heat scan of the area. He then sent some e-mails via his Blackberry and, after he received some replies, he rapidly produced some graphs from his Excel spreadsheet. Finally, he printed a 150-page report on the mini laser printer in his glove compartment, turned to the shepherd, waving the sheaves of paper, and pronounced, 'You have exactly 1,586 sheep.'

'Impressive. One of my sheep is yours,' said the shepherd.

He watched the young man select an animal and bundle it into his car. Then the shepherd said, 'If I can tell you what your job is, will you give me back my sheep?' After a nod of acceptance from the young man, the shepherd announced, without hesitation, 'You're a management consultant.'

'That's correct,' said the young man, impressed. 'How on earth did you guess?'

'It wasn't a guess,' replied the shepherd. 'You drive into my field uninvited. You ask me to pay you for information I already know, answer questions I haven't asked, and you know nothing about my business. Now give me back my dog.'

I now realize there is more than a sliver of truth in that story – but eleven years ago I had a much more idealistic view of management consultancy. In fact, as I left university for a two-month holiday before starting out as a consultant, that idealism was not just about my chosen career; it was replicated in my view of what it would be like to be a Christian in the workplace.

I thought the big challenges of being a Christian were behind me. I thought I was entering the real adult world where there was respect for individuals, where there was no such thing as peer pressure and where people didn't make fun of you for what subject you studied at university. I thought all those student pressures to live a life that didn't honour Christ, or to throw in the Christian towel altogether, were a thing of the past.

Then that delightful illusion crumbled in my mind before I had even dipped a toe into the workplace. That summer I went on a Christian teaching holiday. There was an 18–30s group which I was part of, but one afternoon a friend and I decided to go to the session for the over-30s entitled 'Being a Christian in the Workplace'. I thought I was going to hear about all the amazing ways in which people were making a difference for Christ at work – whole offices being converted, corporations realizing that Christians make the best employees, successful evangelistic courses in the workplace.

I admit I was naive, but eleven years on that seminar still sticks in my mind for a very different reason. It was memorable because it was one of the most depressing events I have ever attended. Ninety minutes of hearing lots of people, mainly men, mainly in their forties and fifties, excusing themselves as to why they weren't able to stand up and be distinct as Christians at work, in their attitudes, in their decision-making and in their conversations – people saying it was acceptable to be full on for Jesus on a Sunday, but to sideline him quietly the rest of the week.

I vowed then and there that I would do all I could not to end up like those men, and to encourage other Christians not to either. And God took my vow more seriously than I thought he would, because, six years ago, I moved from the world of consultancy to the world of the church with a very specific remit – to be the Workplace Minister of a church in London: All Souls, Langham Place. The church has many workplaces in the vicinity – big retail stores, trendy advertising agencies, hard-working charities, efficient engineering firms. The BBC is right next door.

I was a Christian in the workplace. At All Souls, my job was to help others to be Christians in the workplace, and one of my biggest prayers in that job might sound very strange. It was that Christians in the workplace would be like the yucca plant in my garden. Allow me to explain . . .

Space is at a premium when you live in the centre of London, so we were fortunate to have a garden, but if there was a competition for the smallest garden in Britain, we might well have been in the running for a prize. There's a competition for the smallest loo in a pub in Britain – I know because the pub in the village where I grew up won it – but I haven't yet heard of a competition for gardens. Nonetheless, with the square footage of a sandpit, and with walls as high as a double-decker bus, plant life didn't seem too keen on our garden. In fact, every single flower or plant we ever tried to grow in it just wilted.

Apart from our yucca plant.

I loved my yucca plant. He kept on growing and flourishing despite the conditions and despite the lack of attention from us. So I looked at him and longed that Christians would be like him – rather than like all our wilting flowers. My prayer went something like this: 'Lord, please help the Christians who work around here to flourish like my yucca plant. Keep them from wilting in their faith, even when the conditions in their workplaces are as tough as our garden is for plants.' It was a strange prayer, but I hope you get the gist. And I hope you'll see why I am different from the heir to the throne of Britain. Prince Charles talks to his plants about god(s). I talk to God about my plants.

I know my yucca prayer was a big ask. When I look back on my time as a management consultant, I'm fully aware that there were times when I did not honour Jesus in what I said and what I did. As I look around at other Christians I know, I have also seen many wilting in their faith as a result of the pressures of the workplace. Some have rejected Jesus completely. So the aim of this book is purely and simply to try and help you work without wilting in your faith, as you enter the workplace, or as you continue in the workplace throughout the course of your life.

PART 1

WORK IS A TREADMILL

The life cycle of work

It's not just flowers that wilt.

It had all been going so well. I had finally joined the gym. I had been inducted in how to use all the equipment by the woman who looked like an SAS commando. She had given me the exercise regime to which I had to commit. There I stood among the weights and machines, with old football socks, shorts, a baggy white T-shirt with a picture of a large-nosed monkey on it, weedy white legs, even weedier white arms – a picture of gym virginity. It was my first session in this year's plan to get fit. All plans in the millennium had failed so far. But this one, I assured myself, was going to be different.

First stop was a gentle warm-up on the bicycle, followed by a few stretches which I personally felt were superfluous to requirements. But then came the first real test – the rowing machine. How fast could I row 1,000 metres? Off I went like Steve Redgrave on Red Bull, and I completed the task – even if the Steve Redgrave surge did disappear for the last 900 metres. It nearly killed me, but I was dedicated to the cause.

My exercise regime told me that next up was the running machine, and so I clambered onto the treadmill, spent a while pressing buttons to try to get the machine to actually move, and eventually got going with my ten-minute run.

It only lasted three minutes.

There's no easy way to explain this. I wilted. In fact, it was a rather spectacular wilt. I fell off the treadmill. I didn't mean to get cramp in my right calf, nor to forget to hit the red emergency stop button. And so after three minutes of running, I found myself in a heap of agony on the floor. It felt as if I was having a heart attack. I certainly looked as if I was having a heart attack. Yet all the muscle-rippling men and Lycra-clad ladies around me continued in harmony with their machines as if nothing had happened and this sprawled mess on the floor just didn't exist. So much for love thy treadmill neighbour.

There are many Christians who enter the world of work only to find that, over time, their faith wilts due to all the challenges that the workplace brings. For some, their wilting faith is as spectacular and sudden as my wilting on the treadmill. It breaks our Father's heart.

It may seem ages away, but when you retire, whether that is in forty-five years or forty-five days, I long that you will be more intimate with Jesus than you are now, more obedient in pleasing him and more passionate for his name to be honoured. I hope that when retirement comes, you will not have wilted in your faith, but rather will have matured and flourished and been fruitful in your walk with the Lord – at work, as well as outside it. I long that the Holy Spirit would take this book and that he would use it as part of his means of working in your life. I pray that, unlike me on the treadmill, you would start well *and* finish strong.

That's why Part 1 is picturing work as a treadmill. Not because we are like hamsters, bored out of our brains, spinning

on our treadmill (some find work to be permanently mono-
tonous and dull, but it's not intended to be), but because the
life cycle of work resembles a treadmill. After all, each of us
steps onto the treadmill of work, keeps going on it, and then
at some point we step off. But the million-dollar question is
this: how do we do that without wilting in our faith?

1. STEPPING ONTO THE TREADMILL

Day One in the job is scary whoever you are. Extrovert or introvert. Christian or atheist. Brain or brawn. It doesn't matter. As you are about to step onto the work treadmill, you're a bag of nerves.

My first day in the office as a management consultant was in the middle of a sweltering August when people were in danger of passing out on the London Underground due to the heat – and the smell of stale body odour. This meant that by the time I had negotiated the delights of the Northern Line and come up for air, embarrassing sweat patches were beginning to appear on my now not-so-freshly-ironed shirt. Fortunately, I was at the office well before I needed to be, so I was able to make a sweaty beeline for the Gents in the main reception, and then spent about twenty minutes locked in a cubicle with my shirt off, towelling down the dripping sweat with loo paper, while shaking my shirt trying to get the damp patches to disappear. It was not the classiest start to my new job.

Being clueless

Now sweat patches might not be a problem for you, but there are some issues that are much more common concerns for people as Day One approaches. The number one issue that takes up people's mind time as they start a new job is the fear of being clueless. We are petrified that we will be unable to perform as well as we are expected to. We think we won't make the grade; we won't understand all the jargon; everyone else will be far more competent and qualified than we are. We somehow forget that starting out in a job means that we are not actually expected to know every detail about everything. A friend who trained as an architect told me that his chief fear on starting his first job after qualifying was that he knew he 'didn't really have a clue how to do the job'. Yet in further discussion, he admitted that after a few weeks at work, to his surprise, he discovered that he was far better at his job than he thought.

Some jobs – like being an architect – require specific training to be able to get the role. But other jobs don't. For example, if you're going to be a civil servant, a telesales operator, a banker or an office administrator, you don't require any particular training or qualification before starting the job. I didn't require any specific qualification to be a management consultant. As a result, my employer expected me to have some level of incompetence and ignorance to begin with. In fact, in my initial training in the first few weeks, they even told me what to do in a situation where a client demanded to know whether I was up to the job they were paying me to do.

I needed that training. In the first few weeks at my first client – a large investment bank – I was collared by one of the senior bank managers when we were in the lift together, and he asked me straight out, 'You look very young. What qualifies you to be doing this role, and for our bank to be paying huge amounts of money for your services?'

Those sweat marks started reappearing on my shirt very fast. With faltering voice, I replied with the pre-prepared answer I had been told to give. 'I have gone through the rigorous and comprehensive graduate training programme and so am fully qualified for the role I have been asked to perform on this project.' It didn't sound very convincing. I'm not sure he was totally convinced. I certainly wouldn't have been.

Being cold-shouldered
Up there with being clueless is the fear of being cold-shouldered and not fitting in. It's only natural that we want

to make a good impression. We all like to be liked. Sarah is a Christian who recently got a job as the receptionist at a financial PR company. In her words, the organization was very 'old-school – lots of double-barrels and red braces'. She feared not fitting in with people of a very different background from her own, so she found herself speaking in a fake 'posh voice' at work in an effort to be accepted.

Changing our voice may be extreme, but we all fear being cold-shouldered in the environment where we are going to spend the majority of our waking hours. And it is because of this fear that we can find ourselves compromising our faith and not living in a way that would honour our Saviour. James started working as a sports agent recently and he told me how, from the very first week, he really struggled with telling the truth because the culture of his workplace is one where truth is malleable. As I look back to my first week as a consultant, I remember I didn't get roaring drunk, but I know there were a couple of occasions when I had more alcohol than I should have done. Why did I do that? Because I didn't want to be on the outside. I wanted to fit in.

Unlike the fear of being clueless, this fear of being cold-shouldered is a fear that is more marked for the Christian. Whether or not we are weird – and some Christians undoubtedly are – the very fact that we are Christians will make us different from the majority of our colleagues. We will *seem* weird, even if we are not. Our Christianity is naturally something that marks us out as different.

Being a chicken

We know that, whatever else we are doing as we enter our workplaces, we are going there as ambassadors for the Lord Jesus Christ. And because in all of us there is this desire to fit in and not be cold-shouldered, we fear that we will end up being a chicken when it comes to being open about our Christian faith. In most people, a very real battle wages as Day One approaches. On the one hand, there is the realization that there is no apparent need to 'come out' as Christians because we are still able to do our job perfectly well, even if people don't know we are Christians. But on the other hand, there is an obvious real need to tell people we are Christians as an early part of our role as ambassadors for Christ.

My assessment from talking to many Christians in the workplace is that actually there are relatively few immediate negative responses from people when they discover someone to be a Christian. Negative reactions will often come over time for the Christian standing up for Christ at work, but in the pluralistic society we live in, people are generally not aggressively anti-Christian when they first hear of someone's faith. Ian, who works in IT, told me, 'People have a tendency to treat it as though you've told them you like fencing – nice for you, but who cares?' That is frustrating in the long term as we seek to point people to Christ – but in the short term of the first few days at work, it's worth remembering that when people discover you are a Christian, it is unlikely that they will walk away from you and never speak to you again. Unless they find fencing distasteful.

Things to remember

Being clueless. Being cold-shouldered. Being a chicken. These are not the only concerns for a Christian starting out on the work treadmill, but they do remind us that the workplace is a tough environment. For most people, it is far more challenging spiritually than the challenge of being a new student during freshers week.

So apart from wearing a shirt that hides our sweat, what do we need to remember as we step onto the work treadmill

– whether that treadmill is our very first job or, as with my dad, a new job at the age of sixty-nine?

Prepare for the first week

There is no more critical a period than the first week in a job. Those early days set the course for the rest of our time in the company or organization. The way people view us, and the hours we work, are often largely determined in the first week. There are lots of challenges, but there are also lots of opportunities. People will ask questions about us far more readily at the start than once everything has settled down. So it is key to nail our colours to the mast early on concerning our faith in Jesus.

Mark recently changed jobs to work in a hedge fund and when he was being interviewed for the job he deliberately decided to state up front in the interview that he was a Christian and that he was not up for sailing close to the wind morally. He told them he was not worth employing if that was going to be part of the work.

I would suggest praying for an opportunity to let people know you are a Christian in the first week of a new job. Of course, be natural with people. Of course, don't just crowbar the fact that you are a Christian into a discussion about sales strategy. Of course, don't just ram the fact that you are a Christian down people's throats within five minutes of meeting them. But the longer you leave it, the more difficult it is to tell someone you're a Christian.

So get ready before you start the job. Think through how you might explain to someone that you are a Christian. If no-one knows you are a Christian by the end of the first week, there's an easy solution. Week Two. Monday morning. Ask a colleague, 'What did you get up to at the weekend?' Your colleague will tell you their weekend exploits, and if they are polite they will then ask you about yours. And you can tell them what you did, including the fact that you went to church. If they are not polite and so don't ask you, it's still not a problem. You just say, 'Sounds great. Mine was pretty hectic too. I watched the rugby, went to a mate's party and then went to church on Sunday.'

And it's out there – a minuscule squirt of fragrant perfume. It's out there – someone at work knows that there is some connection between you and Jesus Christ. It's out there – and only God knows what will happen next.

Pray for all areas of your life

When I was a management consultant I didn't pray much about things connected to my job. This is the clearest indication to me now that I didn't sufficiently value my work as a ministry in which I was serving God. I would pray for people I worked with and for my future career direction – and I'd encourage anyone else to do the same. But I very rarely prayed about the things I was involved in at work – the presentation, the meeting, the number-crunching in the Excel spreadsheet. My lack of prayer showed up my lack of theological understanding about my work. God was just as interested in the presentation I was preparing as a management consultant as he was in the Bible study I was preparing as a pastor. I may have believed that in the abstract, but functionally and practically, my prayer life demonstrated a very different belief.

Part of my research for this book has meant asking loads of people what their top bit of advice was for Christians about to start their first job. By far and away the most frequent response was: 'Pray.' Dom is a barrister and he wrote this to me in an e-mail:

Pray about your work and your time there! Set aside time to pray in the morning and pray about what lies ahead at the office. Pray as you walk up the steps to work. Pray as you pick up the phone to answer a phone call. Pray before opening a document. And don't just pray about the specifics of the work on your desk, but pray about your witness there too.

So pray about your work. But praise God for your work too. In your workplace, you will find that most people speak about how they are just dragging themselves through to the weekend. According to a recent Gallup poll, one in five workers is 'actively disengaged' from their job and a further three in five are described as 'sleepwalking' through their day.[1] In that kind of culture, it is very difficult not to find ourselves having exactly the same mentality unless we are regularly giving thanks to God – for his gift of work itself, and for the wealth of incidental experience and relationships that come with it.

Pursue a Christian support network

If I was expecting prayer to be the most common response from people in terms of advice for the Christian starting out in work, I was not expecting the second most common response. Time and time again, I was told how it was critical to encourage people to link up with other Christians – and particularly in an environment where work is actively discussed.

One of the hardest things about moving from student life to working life is suddenly finding that it is more of a challenge to have Christian fellowship. Whether it has been the Student Christian Union or a church youth group, up until this point it is likely that you will have been part of a distinct church ministry for your age group. Suddenly that no longer exists: in church terms, you are now a BSRA – a Bog Standard Regular Adult.

So wherever your work is based, look for a church quickly. Make sure the cross is central, the Bible is taught, it is outward looking and a genuine, loving Christian community – but don't expect it to be identical to the church you have come from. If you are working in London, or in another main city centre, investigate whether there is any mid-week ministry for workers organized by a church or group of churches near to where you work. The best place to find out is the TransformWork UK website, www.transformworkuk.org.

If possible, make sure you take part in some form of small group or accountability group where the challenges of being a Christian at work are discussed. When I started out at work, I started a prayer square with three other close Christian friends. Over ten years later, we are still meeting. It has been invaluable to be able to pray with and be accountable to others about all manner of things, including our time spent at work.

Practise being a godly steward of your resources

All we have has ultimately been given to us by God – our time, our money, our gifts. So as you start out at work, as far as possible, work out a wise balance between time at work, time at church, time with friends, time with family and so on. Be wary of work commitments ballooning to such an extent that it becomes impossible to spend sufficient time with friends and family and at church. But also be wary of being so busy at church that you are unable to build meaning-ful relationships with people at work.

Think through the use of your money too. It is very easy to be thoroughly over-excited about suddenly having regular money coming into the bank account that isn't from the government or the parents. Carried away by the novelty, we can find ourselves neglecting to put in place a structure to ensure that our financial giving actually takes place. Your church, and other charities that you support, will greatly appreciate regular, tax-efficient giving from a new member of the workforce.

Participate distinctively at work

Finally, and perhaps most critically, you need to get involved. Your workplace is the environment that God has given you where you are to live and breathe and flourish with him for the majority of your waking hours. If you are in Christ, his Spirit is living in you, empowering you to make a difference for him during that time.

Yet so many Christians, in an effort not to sin, go into the workplace like hedgehogs. They curl themselves up into a little ball. They hibernate from 9am until 6pm and just try to get through the day. They see their work merely as a means to get money in the bank. They do their jobs with as little interaction with their colleagues as possible. They always have an excuse to avoid the office Christmas party.

In seeking not to be hedgehogs, we can of course make the mistake of becoming chameleons – merging into the prevailing culture of our workplaces during the week, and then merging into the prevailing culture of our church when we go there on a Sunday. We can end up changing who we are depending on where we are, always blending in and not being distinctively Christian in any way at all at work. Yet in my observation, there are actually more Christians entering the workplace as hedgehogs than as chameleons.

So from Day One on the work treadmill, we need to see our work as a way in which we can minister for God by participating distinctively for him.

Recap

1. Stepping onto the treadmill

Concerns at the start

Being clueless

Being cold-shouldered

Being a chicken

Things to remember

1. Prepare for the first week
2. Pray for all areas of your life
3. Pursue a Christian support network
4. Practise being a godly steward
5. Participate distinctively at work

Relate

Name: Graham Caskie
Occupation: Insurance broker

When I left university, I had very little time to think about what was going to happen to me. Nothing I had ever gone through would prepare me for what was the biggest culture shock of my life. After four happy years at university in Glasgow, I, like many generations of Scots before me, took the famous 'High Road to England' to start working in the City of London. I finished university on the Friday, moved down to London on the Monday, and then started work on the Wednesday!

Along with the practical issue of being constantly exhausted for the first month or so, by far and away the major change was suddenly having so little free time compared with before. This may seem trivial, but the consequence of such a time loss was the need to be far more disciplined in my own personal devotions. Without this time with God, working is even more of an uphill battle. As Bill Hybels puts it, it really is a case of being too busy not to pray.

Being in the workplace brings its own temptations and difficulties. Within a few weeks I had an issue with a particular male colleague who would not accept the point of view of our team. When I asked my manager's advice on how to deal with this, she simply replied, 'Don't worry, I'll take him out for dinner tomorrow night, I'll get him really drunk, wear a short skirt and tight blouse and then he'll come round!' This may be an extreme case, but I have faced many other challenges as to how to respond as a Christian to these direct affronts on what is right. It is my firm belief that a major part of our calling in the workplace is to be able to influence these types of situations for the better, but it isn't easy and it isn't always popular.

However, all is not bad with work! In my short time working, God has helped me in my work, and I have been very blessed to have had a number of opportunities to share the Christian faith with my colleagues. The best place is nearly always after the question, 'So what did you get up to at the weekend?' When I'm asked this by colleagues, I try not just to say that I do go to church, but also to explain why I go to church. I'm amazed at how interested my colleagues are when I tell them the reasons why. Although this always has to be done with tact and discernment, I try never to let an opportunity go amiss for this purpose. A couple of colleagues have even asked to come to church with me. So it does work sometimes!

Respond

1. What are the key things you need to think through before starting a new job?
2. What do you think are the most likely things to cause you to wilt in your faith as you start out at work?
3. How will you go about praying for your work?

2. KEEPING GOING ON THE TREADMILL

I only lasted about three minutes on the treadmill before wilting physically. But what is the key to not wilting spiritually as we continue on the treadmill of work? We've survived the first few months of the new job – but what about the next year, the next decade, the next five decades? How do we avoid ending up like those men in that seminar I went to when I was twenty-one?

Whose calls do you always take?

Have you seen the film *The Devil Wears Prada*? The main character is Andy (Andrea), played by Anne Hathaway, who is the personal assistant to Miranda Priestley, played by Meryl Streep. Miranda Priestley is a terrifying powerhouse in the fashion industry, a sort of female designer clothing version of Alan Sugar. Andy starts out as a very down-to-earth girl, but is quickly sucked into all the glamour, power and ambition of the fashion world and her career. Hence the title of the film.

In the middle of the film, there's a poignant scene where Andy has an argument with her boyfriend, Nate, because her work is consuming all her time. They're standing outside a restaurant late at night and Nate complains about how she has missed his birthday, how she's constantly late for all their dates and how he hardly ever sees her any more.

She replies, 'But Nate, I didn't have a choice.'

He looks at her as if to say, 'Of course you've got a choice,' and then her mobile phone goes. It's her boss, Miranda Priestley.

As she stands there, she is faced quite clearly with a choice. Outside the restaurant with her boyfriend at 11pm, the choice is very clear – to answer the phone or not.

There's a pause as the phone continues to ring, and then Andy says, 'I'm sorry, Nate,' and she reaches to answer the phone.

Immediately, Nate responds, 'The person whose calls you always take – that's the relationship you are in. I hope you two are very happy together.'

And with that he walks away.

For Andy in the film, her career was the call she always took. Her career progress was the biggest influence on the decisions she made.

But what about us? Whose calls do we always take in life? Who or what are the strongest influences for us when we have a decision to make? That is the crucial issue in terms of keeping going wholeheartedly with Christ as we travel along the work treadmill.

I doubt that those men in the seminar I went to intended to become highly compromised in their faith. I doubt that it was a sudden overnight decision basically to ignore Jesus at work Monday to Friday. But one decision leads to another decision which leads to another decision, and eventually you get to a place a million miles from where you want to be. If God is not the strongest influence in our decision-making, if he is not the one whose calls we always take, then we will end up just like these men.

In the New Testament, we discover that the Bible definition for an idol is any created thing that we are serving in place of the Creator (Romans 1:25). Idols are any thing or person that kick God off his rightful place as number one in our lives. Idols are God-substitutes. They are the calls we always take over and above God.

So it is worth outlining what are the most common idols at work.

Status is a huge idol for many of us, and it was Andy's biggest idol in the film. We want to be in a position of significance and prestige, and we won't let anything or anyone stop us quite literally careering towards our goal. If it means working late all the time, so be it. If it means letting our moral integrity stay at home when we go off to work, so be it. If it means we need to be ruthless and overly aggressive, so be it. Our desire for status is the call we always take over and above God.

The commonest idol in the workplace is *popularity*. Whereas status is probably a bigger idol for those who are high-flyers, popularity is something we all desire. Time and again we can find ourselves taking popularity's call rather than God's call on a situation at work. Margaret Thatcher's words ring true: 'If you just set out to be liked, you would be prepared to compromise on anything at any time.'

The other key idol is *money*. This isn't just an idol when you want to be as rich as the Beckhams. If you will do all you can to have a huge house, or an exotic foreign holiday, or a season ticket to Manchester United, then it means that you will never do anything at work which might put your salary in jeopardy. And it doesn't even have to be that big. Geoff had been working for a London law firm for a couple of years after leaving university, but wasn't enjoying it that much. He was thinking of changing jobs to become a teacher. 'What's stopping you?' I asked him. He responded, 'I quite like being able to drink Tropicana orange juice, rather than Sainsbury's own brand.'

I find the *Sunday Times* test helpful. Currently the newspaper has over a dozen different sections. Look at all the headings of those different sections and determine if any of these have become your idol. Are any of them the call you always take over and above God?

Possibly not 'News Review'.

But 'Style'? 'Travel'? 'Home'? 'Sport'? 'Business'? 'Appointments'? 'Money'?

A plethora of idols compete for our worship – and the thing that makes it so difficult is that the majority of our work colleagues will be bowing down at these altars to various God-substitutes.

How can you always take God's calls?

So how can we ensure that we keep taking God's calls throughout our working lives? It's important because, if we do have an idol, we will undoubtedly find ourselves wilting in our faith as we continue on the work treadmill.

Start well

The Bible gives us a number of examples of individuals who take God's calls at work, even when everyone else around them is bowing down to other idols. Daniel is the most well-known example. As a civil servant in Babylon, he perhaps best exemplifies someone who kept the Lord first throughout the decades of his career. Above all, Daniel is remembered for his night in the lions' den after he prayed to God rather than to the king (Daniel 6). If career, status, popularity or money had been his idol, then he would undoubtedly have toed the party line. But he didn't. So he got chucked to the lions.

And then he was rescued by God.

How old do you think Daniel was when he made this stand? If you look at any Children's Bible, you'll see Daniel pictured as a young man. The reality was very different. Daniel was in his seventies or eighties when he was thrown to the lions. This was a man at the end of his working career, not the beginning.

If you read the book of Daniel, you will discover that he took God's call in this big situation because his working life had been moulded and grounded by taking God's calls in the small situations early on in his career. Early on, Daniel knew when he had to take a stand, such as when he didn't eat the royal food and wine. Taking God's calls on the smaller things early on was the principle which enabled him to take God's call on the big thing later on.

Don't try this at home, but apparently, if you have a pan of boiling water and you throw a frog into it, the frog jumps straight out and survives. However, if you put a frog in a pan of cold water and then put it on a slow heat, the frog slowly gets hotter and hotter, doesn't notice the heat rising and so boils alive.

It can be just the same at work. We can get boiled slowly like a frog in our workplaces. Once we lie on the telephone once, it is so much more likely that we will lie again, and over time we will find ourselves lying more and more frequently and more and more blatantly. Once we keep quiet on our views as a Christian in a conversation at work, it is much harder to speak up the next time. Soon we might find a year or two has gone by and we haven't spoken of anything to do with Jesus Christ to anybody at work at all. It is very easy to find that slowly over time – after a number of years in the workplace – our distinctiveness as a Christian is non-existent. It has been boiled slowly to death like a frog. We've hardly noticed it disappear, but it has evaporated into thin air.

Daniel didn't slowly boil like a frog. He managed not to because his loyalty to God was greater than his loyalty to his work. God's calls were the ones that he always took – right from the word go.

Work well

It is worth noting that putting God before his work did not mean that Daniel lost his focus on the work he had to do. It's not the case that, because his work wasn't his idol, he didn't give it much attention. Quite the opposite, in fact.

At the start of his career, the king says that Daniel and his three friends are far and away his best employees (Daniel 1:19–20). When you fast-forward to the end of Daniel's career, he is still getting outstanding rankings in his yearly appraisals.

> Now Daniel so distinguished himself among the administrators and the satraps by his exceptional qualities that the king planned to set him over the whole kingdom. At this, the administrators and the satraps tried to find grounds for charges against Daniel in his conduct of government affairs, but they were unable to do so. They could find no corruption in him, because he was trustworthy and neither corrupt nor negligent.
> (Daniel 6:3–4)

Of course, not all of us can be as exceptional in our jobs as Daniel was, but we can all work well with trustworthiness, with no corruption and with no negligence. God wants us to be working well. Christians who are sloppy workers and not concerned about the work they're doing are Christians who are wilting spiritually.

Relate to God well

Daniel refused to compromise when everyone else around him was bowing down to other idols. But he is not the only example of this in the Bible. Another prime example is Jeremiah, who would have been an old man when Daniel was young. Jeremiah prophesied in the time of the looming Babylonian invasion in which Daniel was captured and taken to Babylon.

Despite the pressures, Jeremiah managed to keep taking God's calls – above all, because of his relationship with God. Whatever the situation, he shared his struggles with the Lord. Whenever he had a decision to make, he didn't just try to sort out the situation on his own. One of his prayers starts, 'O my Comforter in sorrow, my heart is faint within me' (Jeremiah 8:18). When things were tough, Jeremiah was honest with God and dependent on God to comfort him, help him and keep him on the straight and narrow.

That should be our natural reaction too. At work, we will almost always be in the minority because of our desire to keep going with Christ – just like Jeremiah. At work, we will be tempted not always to take God's calls – just like Jeremiah. If we are going to keep going with Christ at work, we need to cry out to God – all the time, but particularly when our heart is faint and we are feeling the tug of our God-substitutes. Jeremiah cried out to his Comforter. Do we?

Relate to colleagues well

The final way to help us always take God's calls at work is to relate to those around us well. Jeremiah cares for the people around him. He cries out to God for them. He shows compassion to them. His heart aches for them. He loves people. Yet Jeremiah also hates sin (Jeremiah 8:21 – 9:2). Jeremiah models this love of people and hatred of sin so well, but we see it supremely in Jesus. Do you remember what Jesus said to the woman caught in the act of adultery when she was brought to him?

> Jesus straightened up and asked her, 'Woman, where are they? Has no-one condemned you?'
>
> 'No-one, sir,' she said.

'Then neither do I condemn you,' Jesus declared. 'Go now and leave your life of sin.'

(John 8:10–11)

Amazing words from Jesus. He didn't *condemn* the woman, but neither did he *condone* her actions. This is a great model for how we need to relate to our colleagues throughout our working lives. If we find ourselves always condoning people's actions and making out as though we are in total agreement with them, it will be because the idol we worship is popularity. But if we find ourselves always condemning people and our colleagues think we are very self-righteous and uncaring, it will be because the idol we worship is spiritual superiority. Both are very dangerous.

Taking God's calls at work will mean no condemning, but also no condoning. We will need to love those colleagues of ours who won't have anything to do with Christianity. We need to spend time *on* them, crying out to God for them in prayer, and we need to spend time *with* them, caring for them practically as we show them the love of Christ.

It isn't easy. I think of how I tried to relate to all my colleagues as we discussed our love lives – as I heard their stories of one-night stands, sex outside marriage, colleagues moving in with their boyfriend/girlfriend, unfaithfulness and deception. Part of the tightrope I had to walk was thinking through how to show love and concern, while also being clear on what the Bible says about relationships, sex and faithfulness.

Why should you always take God's calls?

How we relate to colleagues about their love lives is not the only thing that's hard. Everything about always taking God's calls is difficult. So we will only be prepared to keep putting

God's calls first when we realize the truth about all the God-substitutes that battle for our devotion.

This is the verdict on God-substitutes according to God, speaking through Jeremiah:

> For the customs of the peoples are worthless;
>   they cut a tree out of the forest,
>   and a craftsman shapes it with his chisel.
> They adorn it with silver and gold;
>   they fasten it with hammer and nails
>   so that it will not totter.
> Like a scarecrow in a melon patch,
>   their idols cannot speak;
> they must be carried
>   because they cannot walk.
> Do not fear them;
>   they can do no harm
>   nor can they do any good . . .

> Tell them this: 'These gods, who did not make the heavens and the earth, will perish from the earth and from under the heavens.'
> (Jeremiah 10:3–5, 11)

God-substitutes are lifeless, powerless and perishing. They topple over in the wind, just like the child's tennis net I had when I was little. In the West, we are generally quick to pronounce this verdict on the worship of gold statues. But we find it far more difficult to see that it is just as crazy to worship career, money or popularity – or whatever section of the *Sunday Times* it is for you.

I think back to a very poignant time in my life when I was just starting out in the workplace. In the space of a month I had two very significant conversations with two of my closest friends. The conversations were separate, but in both we talked about why each friend was not yet a Christian, and what was stopping them from accepting Jesus as their Lord. One friend said his God-substitute was his family. The other said his God-substitute was sport. Yet tragically, by the end of that year, my first friend's parents were divorcing and my second friend's physical well-being had severely deteriorated.

Of course it's not always the case that our God-substitutes perish quite so suddenly or so dramatically as with my two friends. But they will all perish. Our popularity may fade. Our money may dry up. The career that we worship won't last for ever. One day we will be made redundant or we will retire. Whatever our idol is, it will not last for ever.

But God will. 'The LORD is the true God; he is the living God, the eternal King' (Jeremiah 10:10). That's why Daniel and Jeremiah kept going in their faith, despite being in the minority in the workplace.

If we are going to follow their lead, as we keep going along the work treadmill, the calls we always need to take are those of the eternal King.

Recap

---

2. Keeping going on the treadmill

Whose calls do you always take?
God ... or a God-substitute?

How can you always take God's calls?
1. Start well
2. Work well
3. Relate to God well
4. Relate to colleagues well

Why should you always take God's calls?
God-substitutes don't last for ever

Relate

Name: Angela Clifford
Occupation: Community worker

In my first job at a volunteer bureau I was sent on a training course on 'sexuality awareness'. The training was done through group work and I was with about ten other people from the community work sector.

The course leader announced the first task, which was to make a radio-style 'vox pop' on the theme of 'how I lost my virginity' using clips of interviews from each other. It was supposed to be light-hearted and entertaining, and a bit of an ice-breaker for us. It was clearly assumed that everyone had a suitable story to tell and that it would be great fun to share it with a group of strangers.

As a single twenty-something Christian I found this excruciating. I really didn't want to spend my time making a package about people's pre-marital sexual experiences, but neither did I want to be labelled as a prude. My biggest discomfort came from not wanting to admit that actually I wasn't sexually active (and didn't plan to be until I got married). I didn't want to stick out like a sore thumb. Underlying that was the fear that they would think I was really weird. I wanted at least a passing chance of being popular with my new colleagues.

So, did I say something mature, honest and God-honouring about the task? Did I heck. I sank down into my chair, like the coward I was, hoping I wouldn't be chosen to contribute 'my story'.

Sadly I made many compromises in that job for the sake of popularity, but I did eventually 'come out' as a Christian, and was able to let people know some of the things that I stand for. I wish I'd had more courage earlier, because actually being known as the only Christian in that workplace was quite a privilege and a pleasure in the end, and if I'd had more integrity from the start it would have provided some great opportunities to serve Christ.

Respond
1. Who or what are the calls that you are most tempted to take over and above God in your current situation? Status? Popularity? Money? Something else?
2. In what areas of work do you think you might be in danger of 'boiling like a frog' by compromising more and more over time?
3. Jesus doesn't condemn, nor does he condone. Do you find it easy to strike that balance in relating to others at work?

3. STEPPING OFF THE TREADMILL

Some people reading this book will be preparing to embark on their first full-time job, and so catching sight of a chapter about stepping *off* the work treadmill may feel a touch premature. Admittedly, when I started out as a management consultant, one person just didn't bother turning up on Day Three of the job and never came back, and another person almost found himself making a swift exit after an alcohol-induced vomit over the shoes of the head of Human Resources. But generally, as we start out on the work treadmill, we are hoping not to step off it in the immediate future.

Nonetheless, however long we have been in the workplace, there is significant value in considering the main reasons why we might find ourselves stepping off the work treadmill. The four most common explanations for stopping our work are reflection, redundancy, reproduction and retirement. While these cover a huge variety of situations, the four are united by the fact that when we step off the treadmill of work – for whatever reason – we can more clearly discover where our true identity lies. Not where we would like it to lie, in Christ, but where it actually lies.

Reflection
Reflection is when we voluntarily step off the treadmill of work to assess our situation in life and determine whether we are going in the right direction in terms of how we are using the time God gives us.

Claire was a Human Resources officer who was getting frustrated in her job and was certain that she should leave it. But she wasn't at all sure about the right direction to head in, and her work was so all-consuming that she couldn't find the space and time to think things through properly. Trying to determine her new career direction and then act on this, by applying for jobs in a new field or retraining, was too much for her while she was still in her job. So she quit. It was a courageous move, to leave with no new job to go to and without even knowing in what direction she was heading, but it was certainly the right move for her. It allowed her the space to reassess and then apply for a job working in a very different industry.

A time of reflection doesn't always mean a new direction. Alen quit his job working for a high-powered investment bank, took time out for reflection, and then ended up working for another investment bank six months later. For myself, I took a year out from being a management consultant to try to work out whether I should be a pastor or a management consultant. It was a fantastic year. I did a one-year Bible course, but at the end of the year, I was still none the wiser. So I continued by working part-time as a management consultant and part-time at a church. Talk about keeping your options open!

A time of reflection can therefore be a positive time, but there are two fairly obvious dangers. The first danger comes if you have lots of money saved for the reflection time. You can become very lazy. You get up late. You drift. You have no structure to your life. You have no goals. And very quickly a time of refreshment and reflection becomes a time of mental, physical and spiritual stagnancy.

The other danger comes if money is tighter. Suddenly voluntary unemployment becomes an even greater strain and anxiety than if you had remained in your previously strained and anxious job. It was not for nothing that Paul wrote to Titus, 'Our people must learn to devote themselves to doing what is good, in order that they may provide for daily necessities and not live unproductive lives' (Titus 3:14). That is the general principle of Scripture. A defined period of reflection can be a hugely positive experience, but we have been created by God to work and we should look to find meaningful occupation.

Redundancy

Redundancy is very different from reflection. Redundancy is when we *in*voluntarily step off the treadmill of work. We weren't intending to stop working, but our services are no longer required by our employer.

Redundancy is clearly a very painful time. On top of the obvious financial issues can come feelings of low self-esteem. There can often be a real sense of anger at the way that you have been treated by the organization for which you were working. The most important thing of all is to keep yourself occupied. Not all work is paid work. It's often a help for people who have just been made redundant to go and get some voluntary work or help out in their church while they look for a new job. After a while, it is better to have any job that pays money than no job at all, even if it is not your dream job.

Of course, for some people at the start of their working life, the issue may not be redundancy but the difficulty in finding a job in the first place, particularly during an economic downturn. What starts out as a three-month 'time to travel' turns into a twelve-month nightmare of involuntary unemployment. Whatever the exact situation, unemployment is always a challenge. But it does not need to be a catastrophe.

Reproduction

Stepping off the work treadmill to have a baby is obviously more relevant to some than others, although there are now more and more cases where, after the maternity leave, the father is the one who stays at home to care for the child, while the mother goes back to work.

Whoever is the primary child-carer, the challenges are the same. Mornings revolve around changing nappies rather than changing lanes on the commute to work. Afternoons provide the challenge of entertaining your child rather than entertaining your boss. Evenings consist of rocking a screaming baby to sleep rather than rocking on the dance floor at a work social. It's no wonder that the change comes as a bit of a shock.

Some people take to the change like a duck to water. Others react more like a cat to water. Fiona finished her job last year to start the job of being a full-time mum. This is what she said to me: 'One big difference was that instead of having some specific goals by which to measure my achievements, I was thrust into an endless cycle of feeding, changing nappies and trying to get the baby to sleep: any progress was hard to spot. That's been tough at times, because it's shown me how I've often, wrongly, placed my identity in my achievements rather than in Christ.'

Retirement

It happens at different ages and for different reasons, but there comes a time, even if it seems very far off at the moment, when we will all step off the treadmill of paid work for the final time. If, over the years, we have tended to hate our work, then we will be living for our retirement, longing for the time when each day can be spent walking the dog, or refining the golf swing, or lounging by the pool in Tenerife. It's a blissful image. But it is just that – an image. The reality is very different. Financial challenges are an ever-present concern for many, and even for those with enough saved up to live comfortably for decades, the physical challenges of old age become an increasing frustration. Others are very different. They love their work and fear the time when they have to stop, so when retirement comes, suddenly there is this loss of a purpose for living.

What is your identity?

Whether we step off the work treadmill because of reflection, redundancy, reproduction or retirement, a loss of identity is undoubtedly the key challenge. It's fuelled by the fact that whenever we meet people for the first time, almost the first question we ask after we've discovered someone's name is 'What do you do?' As soon as we hear the answer, we are subconsciously ranking that person according to their occupation. 'I'm just a mother,' says the woman on maternity leave, 'but I used to be a lawyer.' Every time we step off the work treadmill, whatever the reason, we so often feel unsettled because we have allowed our identity to be defined by what we do.

A few years ago I bought a book called *Change the World for a Fiver*. It's a book of fifty actions to 'change the world and make you feel good' – things such as learning basic first aid, giving blood, putting your chewing gum in the bin and planting your own Christmas tree (very thoughtfully, the book even came with five Christmas tree seeds). A charity called We Are What We Do produced the book, and I think that name is probably the unspoken motto for so many people in this world, particularly middle-class Westerners. But I am afraid 'We Are What We Do' is a disastrous motto and it causes so much pain. If we step off the work treadmill, and that's our motto in life, then we will inevitably fall to pieces – because, as we leave our job, our identity is suddenly ripped from us.

So who are you? What is your primary identity?

If you are a builder, are you a Christian who happens to be a builder, or are you a builder who happens to be a Christian? If you are a student, are you a Christian who happens to be a student, or are you a student who happens to be a Christian? If you are unemployed, are you a Christian who happens to be unemployed, or are you an unemployed person who happens to be a Christian?

What is your primary identity in life? In *Get a Life*, Paul Valler states, 'To know who you are, you must know *whose* you are.'[1] It's a reminder that our primary identity as Christians should come, not from our job, but from the fact that in Christ we belong to our Heavenly Father.

> How great is the love the Father has lavished on us, that we should be called children of God! And that is what we are!
> (1 John 3:1)

As Christians, if we are getting off the work treadmill, we haven't actually lost anything in our identity – we are still precious children of God. It's so simple, and yet it's so difficult to let that fact truly transform and govern our lives. Of course there will always be some upheaval with a change in circumstances, but if our identity is rooted in Christ rather than in our job, then we will be much better placed to cope when, for whatever reason, we find ourselves stepping off the treadmill of work.

During World War II there was a problem in the coalmines. Wanting to participate more directly in the effort to defend our country, many of the miners were inclined to leave their difficult, thankless jobs in the mining pits and join the army instead. They wanted to be part of something bigger, more glorious and, as they saw it, more meaningful.

This was a problem, of course, because the war effort desperately needed the coal that these miners brought up out of the ground every day. So one day Winston Churchill spoke to the miners and he told them something surprising. He told them that their dirty, grimy jobs were just as important in the war effort as anyone else's.

He asked them to picture in their minds the grand parade that would take place when the work of the war had come to its conclusion and victory finally came. Their children and grandchildren would be watching along the roadside to see all the heroes who had secured their freedom.

First in the parade, Churchill said, would come the sailors of the British Navy, the ones who had fought hard in the grand tradition of the Navy – the same kind of men as the heroes of Trafalgar and those involved in the defeat of the Armada generations before. Next in the parade, he said, would come the pilots of the Royal Air Force, the few to whom so many owed so much, because their skills and bravery, more than any others, had defended England's skies from the dreaded German Luftwaffe. Then the heroes of the Army would march by, men who had stood tall at Dunkirk and who would have taken the battle directly to the enemy.

But at the end of the parade, Churchill said, would come a long line of sweat-stained, soot-streaked men in miners' caps. At that point, someone from the crowd would shout out, 'And where were you lot during the critical days of the struggle?' Then from ten thousand throats would come the proud answer, 'We were deep in the earth with our faces to the coal.'

We are told that there were tears visible on the soot-laden and weathered faces of those miners. They returned to their mining pits with their shoulders straightened and their heads held high because of Churchill's words.

We are often thinking the same thoughts as those miners – particularly when we step off the work treadmill. We get so focused on the pain, dirt or drudgery of our lives that we feel we're not really doing anything significant for the Lord. We feel as if we're stuck in the pit of redundancy or the pit of indecision over what direction to head in with our work. We want to be a part of something bigger, something more glorious, something more meaningful.

The reality is that we already are – but sometimes we fail to realize it.

If we are Christians, whether we are on the treadmill of work or not, we're still children of God. And as children of God, we have plenty to do that is totally meaningful.

> And now, dear children, continue in him, so that when he appears we may be confident and unashamed before him at his coming.
> (1 John 2:28)

> Dear children, do not let anyone lead you astray.
> (1 John 3:7)

> Dear children, let us not love with words or tongue but with actions and in truth.
> (1 John 3:18)

Dear children, whether we are on the work treadmill or not, our identity doesn't change and we are still part of something huge, something glorious and something meaningful.

Recap

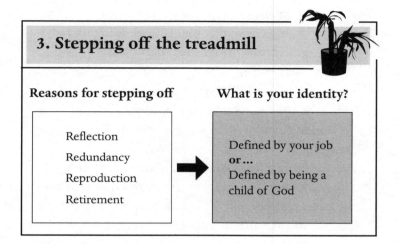

3. Stepping off the treadmill

Reasons for stepping off

Reflection
Redundancy
Reproduction
Retirement

What is your identity?

Defined by your job
or ...
Defined by being a
child of God

Relate

Name: Jeremy Meyer
Occupation: Currently doing a church apprenticeship

In May 2006 I started a job with a sales and marketing
agency. I was headhunted into the role. Three months
later at my review meeting I was asked to leave.

It is not easy to cope with a situation like that. Yes, I
needed healing from being rejected, also from my desire
to want to blame my boss and others for my situation,
and also healing so that I could find the motivation to
move on and get another job. God graciously provided
all of this.

My biggest challenge while out of work was figuring
out what to do next job-wise, keeping busy and keeping
the momentum up while regaining my confidence. In
my line of work, recruitment consultants can be very

helpful, so there was always hope and opportunity. Perhaps the strangest experience was collecting the dole while being conscious that others doing likewise were facing far harder situations than I was.

While I was out of work, I got huge reassurance from my church family, my homegroup and others who prayed for me. When you let him help you, God has a wonderful way of creating motivation when you are battling.

After four months, I landed a great job with the Nut Company where I account-managed Tesco. A year and a half later, I left the job. This time it was my decision. I decided to take up an apprenticeship at a church. About eight months into my role at the Nut Company I had a real sense that something had to change. I was pretty much flat out at work and I felt a strong desire to channel my energies into some sort of church work, and the apprenticeship scheme at my church enabled me to explore this further. The hardest things about making the decision included moving into shared accommodation, losing my car and eating into a good chunk of my savings. The apprenticeship pays no salary, but there is a small grant which definitely helps. As I see it now, I am taking a year out. Time will tell what happens next.

Since becoming a Christian three years ago, I have learned to lean on the Lord more and more at work. Being out of work is a real challenge and regular prayer has been critical to maintain focus and avoid distractions and temptations. For now, the challenge is to work with people, rather than products, while receiving less financially and being challenged more spiritually.

Respond

1. Do you find it easy to know that your fundamental identity is not defined by what you do?

2. Whether you are working or stepping off the work treadmill, you are part of something huge, glorious and meaningful. How does that make you feel?

3. If you are starting out in the world of work, how can you make sure that your identity remains defined by being a child of God rather than by your job?

PART 2

WORK IS A TRAMPOLINE

The highs and lows of working life

Hopefully, picturing work as a treadmill has been a help. The danger of that image, however, is that work can be seen to be a bit too predictable. We start working, we keep working and we stop working. That's it. We've got the standard life cycle of work sussed. But as you will know if you've been in the workplace for any length of time at all, it's far more dynamic than that. Sometimes too dynamic.

First, the *world of work* is dynamic. Sixty years ago, people expected to have a job for life. You chose your treadmill, stepped onto it, and kept going until you retired. Not any more. It is now estimated that a typical member of Generation Y (born after 1982) will have had ten jobs by the age of thirty-eight.[1] Stepping off one treadmill and onto another one is an ever more frequent event.

Second, the *economy* is dynamic. When I started as a management consultant, it was the beginning of the dot-com boom. Everything was rosy. Money was flowing everywhere. We used to get taken out for team meals at smart restaurants almost every week. Five years later, when I moved from being a management consultant to work in a church, hundreds of people in the office were being made redundant on the same day because the dot-com bubble had burst. Now it's even worse – we're gripped by all the fears that a full-blown recession brings.

Third, *organizations* are dynamic. Changes happen. It might be a merger. It might be a change of strategy. It might be a change of policy. Five years ago, a newly qualified doctor in the UK was pretty much guaranteed a job in the National Health Service because there were more jobs than doctors. Last year, newly qualified doctors were scrambling for jobs because there are now more doctors than jobs. More and more people are being encouraged to train as doctors in this country and a greater influx of doctors are coming into the UK from overseas. Things change.

Fourth, *relationships* are dynamic. I think of Roger, with whom I used to work. He used to find it very difficult because he didn't get on with our boss at all. He would constantly get low-ranking appraisals. He was miserable at work. But then his boss changed, and the new boss respected Roger hugely for the quality of his work and his attitude and his skills.

Fifth, *we* are dynamic. Our desires for our work at one moment in time may be very different at another moment. For example, in our twenties we might prefer to work long hours in exchange for breaks to go travelling, but in our thirties we may want to reduce our hours or have greater flexibility in how and when we work to fit in with family responsibilities. Or our desire for the type of job we do can change. I can think of plenty of friends who are now in completely different jobs from those they originally started after their studies: the business analyst who is now running an art gallery; the engineer who now sells handbags; the shop assistant who is now a postman; the teacher who is now working in the Foreign Office.

It is because of all these different springs of dynamism that the trampoline is a good image for work. Work is not predictable, but full of instability, uncertainty and change. So many ups and downs. So many high points and low points. So much to do. So much to think about. So difficult to feel any sense of balance and control. So much fear of flying off in the wrong direction at any moment. As Christians, we need to learn how to be a part of this wildly undulating world of work and yet not wilt in our faith.

4. KEEPING YOUR BALANCE

If you are not able to keep your balance, life on a trampoline gets very messy. Yet balance is also one of the first things that needs mastering when we enter the workplace. The Work Foundation defines work-life balance as being 'about people having a measure of control over when, where and how they work, leading them to be able to enjoy an optimal quality of life'.[1] It's an issue that's climbing up the agenda for everyone. For example, recent UK graduate careers surveys show that graduates now value flexibility more than pay when looking at prospective employers.[2]

Work-life balance is a big issue. It is also a big challenge. In the UK, we work the longest hours in Europe, we eat the most ready meals and we even drink faster than our neighbours. One recent survey found that many of us use high-tech gadgets so that we are able to get thirty-one hours of work out of a twenty-four-hour day.[3] Work-life balance is clearly not an easy thing to achieve, but we need to have it under control if we are going to work without wilting in our faith.

You may be surprised, therefore, that in this chapter I'm not going to address work-life balance at all. Not because it's not relevant, but because I believe it's an unhelpful term. By calling it a 'work-life balance', we make it sound as though work and life are distinct and separate from each other. It creates in us the impression that if you have more work, then you must have less life. This is patently untrue. Work is not the opposite of life, but a subset of life. Even though there are times when it might feel like it, it's not true that if you have more work, then you have less life.

It is far more profitable to think about our 'life balance' – how we can manage all the different tasks and responsibilities we have in life. Satisfactorily juggling all the different balls in life, without spilling them or causing serious damage to ourselves or others – that's the trick. For a lot of people, however, the problem is that work is just one ball too many.

Recently I asked a group of about fifty Christians in the workplace whether they thought they worked (a) too few hours, (b) about the right amount of hours, or (c) too many hours. The results were revealing. No-one said they worked too few hours; 40% thought they worked about the right number of hours; and 60% considered they worked too many hours.

So why – if you're one of the 60% – do you agree with the majority of workers and feel you work too many hours? Demands from the boss? Pressing deadlines? The long hours culture in your workplace? The fear of being fired? All those are genuine reasons. But maybe there are issues underlying those reasons which cause us to work not just long hours, but too many hours week after week after week.

Crucial misunderstandings

I wonder if you've read this article before.

> The Advertising Standards Commission has rejected a complaint lodged by Bob Weller of Carlisle against Beechams Pharmaceuticals regarding claims made on the packaging of their 'Mr Muscle' product. According to the adverts, kitchen and bathroom cleaner Mr Muscle 'Loves The Jobs You Hate', but Mr Weller says that this is just not the case.
>
> Mr Weller said, 'I took a bottle of Mr Muscle into the office where I work as a chartered accountant on a day when

I had some particularly tedious jobs lined up. Firstly, I'd been asked to prepare a quarterly sales summary for a client in Ramsgate. I expected this to take most of the morning, so I sprayed the keyboard of my computer with a liberal coating of Mr Muscle and went to the toilet where I slept until 11.30. Now, compiling quarterly summaries for large companies is one of the worst things about my job, I hate it in fact, so I'd expected Mr Muscle to have done a great job because he loves the jobs you hate. Yet I was astonished when I returned to my desk and discovered that he hadn't even started!

'That afternoon I was scheduled to interview graduates for a junior position with the firm. If there's one thing I hate more than quarterly summaries, it's interviewing students, so I again decided to leave it to Mr Muscle. I squirted him all over the conference room on the second floor, left the bottle on the table and asked my Secretary, Miss Harris, to usher in the candidates when they arrived. When I returned from the pub about four hours later, I was sure Mr Muscle would have at least prepared a short-list for a second interview. But had he indeed! He was on the table where I'd left him, had taken no notes whatsoever and all of the students had gone. I was furious!' continued Mr Weller.

Jon Ramsey of the Advertising Standards Commission said in a statement, 'Bob Weller is a nutter. Mr Weller has been sacked by his company and has a number of complaints to the Advertising Standards Commission awaiting review, including one against Cadbury Confectionery, claiming that he has yet to find romance with a female rabbit, despite eating forty Caramels in one week.'

Now Bob Weller totally misunderstood what Mr Muscle is all about. He completely missed the point. We laugh at his complete and utter stupidity. We know that none of us could possibly be that stupid. But my fear is that actually many of us are. I know I often am.

We often totally misunderstand something far more important and far more significant than Mr Muscle. In fact, far too often we misunderstand two things: our work and ourselves. This has devastating consequences for our life balance, because, as with Bob Weller, wrong thinking leads to wrong action.

Misunderstandings about our work

It is at the interaction between our employment and our working for Jesus that the misunderstandings come – misunderstandings over where, how and when we work for Jesus.

Where we work for Jesus

You can work for Jesus in your day-to-day work. This may sound obvious, but it is worth stating, because this truth doesn't always come across in church. Mark Greene, writing to church leaders, comments, 'There is a danger that we will view church members exclusively in terms of how they can contribute to the church in the neighbourhood, rather than how they might contribute to the growth of the kingdom of Christ, wherever he has placed them.'[4] How I wish there were more church leaders who would take this comment on board. So often people are prayed for regularly for the one hour a week when they are a Sunday school leader – but they never receive prayer for the fifty hours a week they spend in their jobs. When I was working at All Souls, we introduced a Workplace Sunday and as part of the day we asked everyone who was in a workplace to stand up to be prayed for and commissioned in their ministry at work. As I talked with people afterwards, I reckoned that this one act had more of a positive impact on encouraging people to serve Jesus in their workplaces than any sermon on work that I ever preached.

So we need to be thinking rightly about where we can work for Jesus in our lives. It may cause us to work longer hours in our workplaces when we realize we are working for Jesus at work. But that may be right, because we can serve Jesus at work just as much as we can serve him anywhere else.

How we work for Jesus

Some people work too many hours. They excuse their long hours at work by saying they are working for Jesus by doing a good job. It is a half-truth. To be working well for Jesus in our workplaces we do need to be doing as good a job as we possibly can – working hard for our bosses. But that is not the sum total of it. If our mentality is that the only way to serve Jesus at work is to do well and get promoted fast and be known to be the best at what we do, then our life balance will come unstuck because we will spend far too long in our workplaces. This is one aspect of serving Jesus at work, but it is not the only aspect. Matters of integrity, ethics, witness, character and attitude are all just as important as doing as good a job as we possibly can. So too is how we work for Jesus in all the other areas of our lives.

When we work for Jesus

I've come across people with the mentality of 'I'll work flat out now and then in a few years I'll pull back and I'll have more time for serving Jesus then', or 'I'll work flat out now and not be too focused on Jesus in my job, but in a few years' time I'll be in a real position of influence and I can make a difference for Jesus then'. Again, that is wrong thinking. After all, Jesus said, 'If anyone would come after me, he must deny himself and take up his cross *daily* and follow me' (Luke 9:24). Each and every day we need to be looking to be full-on, wholehearted followers of Jesus wherever we are. There is no time out from being someone who works for Jesus.

Misunderstandings about ourselves

Our life balance is kicked off-balance by having the wrong view of our work, but it is also tipped up by our wrong view of ourselves. Ephesians 2:10 gives a great summary of the right view that we should have of ourselves as Christians. Paul writes that 'we are God's workmanship, created in Christ Jesus to do good works, which God prepared in advance for us to do'.

- This verse tells us about our *identity*: that we are God's workmanship, his work of art, literally his masterpieces.
- This verse tells us about our *value*: that we are created in Christ Jesus. We are so valuable and precious to God that he sent his only Son to die for us.
- This verse tells us about our *purpose*: that we are to do good works for God.

Too often, most of us have a huge misunderstanding about our identity, value and purpose, and this has a significant impact on our life balance by causing us to work longer hours than we should. I know this was a challenge for me at All Souls. Let me explain.

At times I suffered from an identity problem. I saw myself first and foremost as an Associate Minister at All Souls, Langham Place. That was who I was, not God's workmanship. At times I suffered from a value problem. I got my value and self-worth not from the fact of Jesus dying for me and rescuing me, but from wanting people to think I was a relatively young but relatively successful pastor and Bible teacher. At times I suffered from a purpose problem. I thought my purpose was to try to give as many good talks and put on as many good events as possible, rather than to do good works for God's glory. And all of those problems combined to contribute to my working longer hours than I should have done.

But I don't think it's just me. When our identity is wrapped up in our job and our status, when our value comes from the size of our pay packet or the comments on our annual appraisal, when our purpose is defined only in relation to our job and our career progression – it is then that we are likely to be skew-whiff in our life balance.

That's not to say that we will never be busy at work if we are clear on our identity, value and purpose as Christians. After all, the 'good works, which God prepared in advance for us to do' might include providing food for our family, or ensuring that we are an integral part of the team we work with so we earn the right to share our life and our Lord with them, or working to keep the business afloat and people's jobs in existence. All of those are good works for God – and they may cause us to work long hours. But too often our purpose at work is far more egocentric, and that drives us to work not just long hours, but too many hours. Sometimes a sixty-hour working week is just what God wants us to be doing. It can be a good and right life balance at a certain moment in time, but sometimes it isn't, and right thinking about our work and ourselves is the first step to help us maintain good balance in our lives. If you want to think through this issue in more depth, Paul Valler's book *Get a Life*, which is part of this 'Faith at Work' series, is a great place to start.[5]

Busy or too busy?
It's true that many of us are working long hours; getting into work early and staying at work late; taking work home;

working weekends. It's true that, according to the *Guardian* newspaper, only 43% of people in the UK take a break at lunchtime. We are busy at work.

We're not just busy at work, though. We're busy socializing too. Church also takes up time. I spoke to someone recently and discovered he was attending a church meeting every single night of the week.

One of my colleagues at All Souls, Rico Tice, often repeated the mantra, 'The urgent is the enemy of the important.' He was right. We are so busy, we don't give ourselves time to think about things that are really important. Take relationships. I know someone who was made redundant recently. He's in his forties. He told me that in some ways he was glad that his job had finished because he could now actually begin to look for a wife. He hadn't had time before. Or take friends. Regularly I try to meet up with someone and we can't find a free date closer than three months away. Or perhaps most criticially, take our relationship with Jesus. Someone recently said to me, 'I'm go, go, go all day and then I just speak to Jesus in prayer for five minutes at midnight in my bed before falling asleep.'

All these are reasons why I can believe what I read in one of the free newspapers that are handed out at tube stations in London – that half of all adults in this country say they are constantly tired. At times we will be busy, and that is not necessarily wrong. Being a full-time mum with two small children has meant that my wife is busier and more exhausted now than she ever was when she worked in Human Resources for a law firm. But there are times when many of us are too busy.

So it is important that at any point in life we assess our right responsibilities in terms of family, church, friendships, physical exercise, relaxation and personal time with God, as well as our right responsibilities in work. In fact, in his brilliant book *The Busy Christian's Guide to Busyness*, Tim Chester help-fully points out that more often than not, the pressure to be too busy comes not from without, but from within.[6] I noticed this particularly when reading an article in the *Evening Standard* magazine on busyness. Here are three reasons for being busy that were given by people in the article.

1. 'Busy makes you feel smug; it makes you feel powerful and wanted. It makes you feel, in short, like a G8 leader popping out of the auditorium to tackle another world crisis . . . Busy is the cocaine of the 21st century.'
2. 'I need busy to feel good, and when I don't have busy, I feel lost, so I need to get even busier in order to feel good again.'
3. 'Being busy prevents you from worrying about yourself . . . It allows you not to consider big things, such as what is the purpose of your life.'[7]

Fundamentally, the reason for being too busy in all three of those quotes has to do with what is going on in these people's hearts. The heart of human busyness is the busyness of the human heart. It's why, in his book, Tim Chester challenges each of us to identify the desires of our heart that make us try to do more than God expects of us.[8] It could be the desire to prove ourselves, or to please people, or to be in control, or to hide from difficult issues, or to be fulfilled by possessing more and more. Whatever these desires of our heart are, they become obvious because they eventually cause harm to our bodies and health, or to our relationships with family and friends, or to our church commitments, or above all to our relationship with God.

If being too busy is your danger, it might be worth buying and reading a copy of Tim Chester's book. It has made a huge impact on many people I know – including me.

Changing the trampoline

This chapter has outlined the idea that the ability to have a good and godly life balance is dependent on two strategies. First, if we get our thinking right about ourselves and our work, then we will be in our workplaces for about the right number of hours. And second, if we identify and modify the desires of our heart, then we will not be too busy in our lives. Taken together, these two strategies will enable us to balance well on the trampoline of work. That's the theory – but putting it into practice is more difficult.

Probably the most common pastoral workplace question that I have been asked by people over the last six years has been: 'How do you know when it's time to change jobs?' Generally this is asked as a result of the person struggling to develop a satisfactory life balance. The struggle, stress and difficulty of having a 'life outside work' all contribute to a feeling that the only way to obtain life balance is to change the work trampoline altogether.

So what should our checklist be in deciding whether to leave our current job and start a new one?

Character

The number one reason for changing our job is that our current job is having a long-term negative impact on our character as a Christian. There will always be times when we stuff up at work – when we don't act as Jesus would want us to. But if this starts being a regular thing, and it is particularly because of the nature of the job we have, then it is time to hand in our resignation. If we find ourselves constantly lying to clients because 'that's the way it works', or if we regularly become involved in unethical practices because 'that's the only way to make money', or if every Friday we end up having too much to drink because 'that's the culture of the office', or if we continually work till midnight and at weekends so that our relationship with God suffers because 'that's part of the deal with the job', then we need to look to move to a new job where we will be able to operate in a Christ-pleasing way. Often, when we are far too busy in our work, it's more likely that our character as a Christian will suffer. The way we work is of far greater significance than the job we do.

Competency

The second reason for getting a new job is competency. If we realize that we are not able to do the job well, and over a continuous period of time it is causing us huge stress or causing us to be constantly reprimanded, then it is sensible to look to move jobs to something more compatible with our giftings. This may make us feel as if we have failed – but we have not. It is far better to be in a job where we are able to conduct ourselves in a manner worthy of Jesus, than to struggle for years and years growing bitter, stressed and frustrated.

For others, changing job will be a move to something that is more challenging and stretching. If we are bored with our job, it will tend to have a negative impact on our influence for Christ at work. We need to assess other factors before jumping ship as soon as there is the first whiff of boredom – after all, no job will be totally fulfilling. But it is not wrong to look to move to a job that uses some of the gifts God has given us.

Colleagues

Our colleagues are the people with whom we spend most time in life. It is likely that for most of our colleagues, we are the only Christian they know. God in his sovereignty has 'determined the times set for them and the exact places where they should live. God did this so that men would seek him and perhaps reach out for him and find him' (Acts 17:26–27). And not just the exact places where they live, but the exact places where they work too. So we should think hard about the relationships we have formed with our colleagues, and our role in pointing them to Jesus, before we leave for a new job. If we are constantly moving from one job to the next, we will never form the kind of close friendships with our colleagues which can be a powerful vehicle for sharing our lives and, with our lives, the gospel.

Calling

In the Bible, we read that we are called supremely to Christ (Romans 1:6). As part of that, we are called to be holy and to suffer. This means that when we talk about being 'called' to a particular job, it is actually a very minor subsection of our whole calling as a Christian. Nonetheless, all of us do need to see our work as part of the way we serve God within our supreme calling as Christians, and that may mean looking to move jobs.

However, generally when we talk about being 'called' to a particular type of work, all we really mean is that God has wired us up in such a way that we have a particular passion and interest for that type of work. That's fine, but our personal passions and interests cannot be the only things that guide us in terms of what job we do. The truth is that it is not our right to have a job that is fulfilling. Yes, it is a blessing if we enjoy our job (Ecclesiastes 3:13), but work will often be frustrating. In fact, the reality is that it is a huge luxury to have any choice over what job we do at all. For the majority of the world's population, there is no real choice – just an urgent necessity to have any job to earn some money.

Cash

It's not wrong to change jobs because another job is better paid. It's not wrong to earn lots of money. By having an increased salary we are better able to provide for ourselves and our dependants, for the poor, and for gospel ministry through our local church and other organizations or individuals. But we need to weigh this against the increased time and increased responsibility that generally comes with an increased salary, and consider how this will affect our life balance in terms of commitments outside work. Also, if the increased salary is the only reason we are moving job, it is unlikely to be a good enough reason to move. If all that excites us about the job is the sum coming into our bank account each month, then we will find ourselves loving money and hating our new job – which is a recipe for disaster.[9]

Whatever the trampoline . . .

At the end of the day, as much as we may feel that it is critical that we are in the 'right' job for us, the specific work trampoline on which we find ourselves bouncing is not the most important thing. Far more important is that, in whatever job we do, we manage to cultivate a life balance which encourages us to live godly lives both inside and outside our work. John Piper has perhaps summarized it best when he writes, 'You don't waste your life by *where* you work, but by *how* and *why*.'[10]

Recap

4. Keeping your balance

Misunderstandings about our work
⇥ About **where**, **how** and **when** we work for Jesus

Misunderstandings about ourselves
⇥ About our **identity**, **value** and **purpose** as Christians

Busy or too busy?
⇥ Check the desires of our heart

Changing the trampoline
1. Character
2. Competency
3. Colleagues
4. Calling
5. Cash

Relate

Name: Mary Currie
Occupation: NHS manager

What are your priorities in life and how do they govern your career decisions? I left school, studied a geography degree and was left with the question, 'What next?' I had been a Christian for a number of years and wanted actively to seek God's will for my future. Spending some time abroad and serving God in a very different situation were both attractive and so for the next two years I taught with Voluntary Services Overseas (VSO) in north-eastern Nigeria, where letters took three weeks to arrive from the UK. God taught me a great deal about relying on him, studying his word and reaching out to others.

I returned to the UK in 1974 and joined the staff of UCCF, working with students in London and south-east England. It was a real privilege seeing God working in individuals' lives, seeing them grow in their knowledge and love of him and their desire to serve him, but again after four years I was left with the question, 'What next?' Should I continue in 'full-time' Christian work? I was offered a job at the Round Church in Cambridge, but was still uncertain as to whether this was really God's direction. As a UCCF staff worker, I had missed interacting and building longer-term relationships with non-Christians and I sensed that God was leading and calling me to serve him as his ambassador in the secular world. But where?

For the past thirty years I have been working in a variety of managerial roles within the National Health Service. God has been very gracious in giving me both opportunities for career progression and stimulating roles. As I have changed jobs and taken on new roles, a number of factors have governed my decisions:

- My desire to serve God in all aspects of my life and to make a difference wherever God puts me.
- To be an ambassador for him, demonstrating his character, bringing integrity into the workplace and a concern for individuals with whom I work and manage.
- A concern to ensure that I maintain a balance in my working life that enables me to play an active part in my church and still have time for family and friends.

- A recognition that career, status and position in a work structure is not the be-all and end-all of life.

So how has this worked out in practice? It has meant not applying for certain posts that would require being resident on call or attending many evening meetings, or where bringing work home to do at weekends would be the expected norm. Twelve years ago, when I was churchwarden, I took a conscious decision not to apply for executive/board-level jobs, realizing that for me they were just not compatible with the other priorities and responsibilities in my life. God has been amazingly faithful. I have a stimulating senior-level post where I have negotiated a flexible working arrangement to enable me to have time to fulfil other responsibilities, such as being part of the UCCF Trust Board, being heavily involved in my church, and having the time and energy to use my home in the service of Christ.

Respond

1. Is your 'life balance' currently out of kilter? As you look ahead, are there particular changes happening in your life that may damage your life balance?
2. Can you 'identify the desires of your heart' that are making you do more than God expects of you?
3. What factors would most influence you in deciding to change jobs?

5. SURVIVING THE UPS AND DOWNS

Trampolines are obviously full of ups and downs. So is work. Whether it is due to the economic climate, our personal performance or our relationship with the boss, there are plenty of reasons why we can find our circumstances altering as we go through our working life. Both up times and down times at work provide their own unique challenges to our faith.

When you are on the up . . .

It was that smooth man of chat, Michael Parkinson, who got me thinking. He was interviewing Nigella Lawson – she who is known as the Domestic Goddess – on his Saturday night show. He ventured to suggest that Nigella was very ambitious. The Goddess was rather offended. 'I've never been ambitious,' she retorted, 'but I need to have a purpose.'

When you look in dictionaries for the definitions of 'ambition' and 'purpose', they are remarkably similar. Both definitions centre around the idea of an eager and strong desire to achieve something. Yet in Nigella's eyes, while purpose is an absolute necessity, she just doesn't do ambition.

As Christians, we're much the same. Take a moment to reflect on the title of the best-selling book by Rick Warren, *The Purpose Driven Life*.[1] We're not all buying copies of *The Ambition Driven Life*, are we? 'Ambition' is a dirty word. 'Purpose' comes with a holy glow.

Or take someone I met who worked in the political arena. One of his colleagues had said that he was 'the most ambitious person in the office', and he was devastated. He felt a failure – as though he had let Jesus down. But if he had been told he was a person of great purpose, I'm sure his reaction would have been very different. Even the apostle Paul tells the Philippians to be one in purpose, but to do nothing out of selfish ambition (Philippians 2:2–3). Christians, it seems, are with Nigella. We don't want to be known as ambitious, but we're all for a bit of purpose.

So how should we act when things are on the up in our work? Is it wrong to be ambitious for success? And how should we deal with the success if it comes our way?

Take Joseph – the one with the famous technicolour career. Consider the facts. After being sold to slave-traders by his brothers, he became a servant to Potiphar, an Egyptian government official. From there he eventually ended up as prime minister of Egypt, via a stint behind bars after he was accused of attempted rape. He was a godly, ambition-driven worker if ever there was one. For sure, it was a rollercoaster ride, yet all the time he showed godly ambition, even as a servant.

Ready to shine for God

It is worth pointing out that there is nothing wrong with being successful. It is great if you are successful in your career or your job. In his first job, Joseph was graded 'exceptional' in his first three-month review meeting with his boss, Potiphar. In fact, he was so successful that he was promoted way ahead of schedule, and put in charge of everything Potiphar owned (Genesis 39:3–4).

So there is nothing wrong with being successful in our job, but there is everything wrong with taking the credit for success. It's very easy at work, if we are successful, to take all the credit for ourselves. Rather than giving the glory to God, we put our success down to luck, fortune or, most commonly, to working hard. The preacher Charles Spurgeon used to say, 'Never praise secondary causes.' God is the ultimate source of our abilities that enable us to get a promotion or to be successful. He is the primary cause.

It is striking that Joseph obviously makes sure that he doesn't take the credit for his success. Joseph's bosses always know that it is the Lord who has given Joseph his success (see Genesis 39:3, 23 for two examples). Presumably that is because Joseph was at pains to point out that the Lord was the primary cause of all his success. He wasn't shy about speaking of the Lord. He was ready to shine, not for himself, but for God.

A couple of years ago I went to hear a lecture given by someone I know. We used to help on the same Christian holiday camps. This guy is now pretty famous. He was giving a lecture at this grand place in London about what he had been up to, and it was amazing to hear. Yet I was saddened because, as he spoke about all he had accomplished, there was no recognition that God was in ultimate control, helping him with his achievements. It was a great opportunity for my friend to give public praise to the Lord, but he did no such thing. I fear ambition had taken something of a grip on him, and as a result he was shining not so much for God, but rather for himself.

That was my friend in quite a public situation – but what about me and you in our workplaces? Not so public, not so famous, but just as important. Are we willing to shine for God? I know, as I think back to my time as a management consultant, that there were times when I wasn't willing. Times as simple as when as a colleague asked me why I seemed calmer than most other people, and I just shrugged my shoulders in a 'trying to be humble way' and said little, rather than explaining that it was because I could rest assured that Jesus was in ultimate control.

That is the challenge for each one of us if we experience success in our jobs, whether success means an outstanding annual review, hitting your sales target, getting a contract for your band with a big record label, or just seeming calmer than most in the office. Do we say, 'It's all down to me and my hard work'? Or do we give God the credit? Joseph's pagan boss recognized the Lord behind Joseph's success. Does your (neo-pagan?) boss see the Lord behind your successes at work? Does your boss even know that you are a Christian?

Joseph's ambition was for God's promotion. Yet it's so easy for our ambition to be for our own promotion. Joseph was ready to shine for God. Are we?

Refuse to sin against God

Joseph was the kind of guy all the girls wanted to be with and all the guys wanted to be. Not only was he as successful as he could possibly be within the sphere of his job, but he was also 'well-built and handsome' (Genesis 39:6). Joseph had it all. He was successful, sturdy and sexy – and his boss's wife saw that and wanted a piece of the action. It's said that opportunity only knocks once, but temptation leans on the doorbell. That's what Joseph experienced. Day after day, his boss's wife tried to persuade him to go to bed with her.

It will be similar for all of us in our different workplaces. The temptation to sin may not come in the form of sexual temptation, but there *will* be huge temptations to sin and they will be huge because the temptations are packaged as appealing offers. Perhaps it's an offer that will bring us greater success, popularity or status at work – but it's an offer that will involve us sinning, whether that means conveniently agreeing to forget to follow health and safety regulations because it saves money, or the pressure to fiddle the company's tax return, or encouragement not to keep confidential something that is supposed to be kept private. The temptation will be different for different people. Yet for all of us, it will be a relentless assault tempting us to cave in. Temptation will be leaning on our doorbell.

Joseph's doorbell was ringing and yet, despite the persistent pleading and flattery of Potiphar's wife, he would not be drawn into sin. He knew that refusing this request from the boss's wife was unlikely to be beneficial to his career, but he stood firm. He refused to sin against God.

Joseph demonstrates that for Christians there is to be no compromise. He does everything he can to avoid sin. He even ends up running out of the house naked, fleeing the seductress, so determined is he to avoid falling into sin.

Take Lucy. She recently finished being in the cast of one of the most well-known West End musicals, and was then offered a leading role in a brand-new musical. It would have been one of her biggest roles yet. But she made the tough decision to turn the part down because of some of the things she would have to do, say and wear as part of the musical, and because of the overall message that this musical communicated. It was a tough decision for her, but she knew she had to put godliness above success. She, like Joseph, knew she had to care more for her purity than for her prospects.

Linked to 'no compromise' is 'no compartmentalization'. As Joseph tells his boss's wife why he won't sleep with her, he mentions two reasons. He says that it would be an offence against his boss – an abuse of the trust placed in him. He also recognizes that it would be an offence against God.

Joseph refused to compartmentalize his life. He knew that any sin, in any area of his life, was not just an offence horizontally with other humans, but also an offence vertically with God. And that's why he refused to sin, even when that refusal could result in a hugely detrimental effect on his career, on his status, and on his standing in society.

It's fine to be successful at work, but it is not fine to sin to get there.

Recognize the sovereignty of God

As Joseph's career continued on from these successful beginnings, he met both success and failure in worldly terms. He ended up in prison for a long stint as a result of rejecting the advances of Potiphar's wife. But wind the clock on thirteen years, and he finds himself with the power of Pharaoh. At the age of thirty, he's got the royal credit card (Pharaoh's signet ring). He's got the designer clothes. He's even got an A-list celebrity wife, the daughter of the most powerful priest in the land. He's a somebody – not a nobody. Yet still he looks to shine for God and not sin against God.

We can see that particularly clearly in two specific instances in his life. The first is in the way he treats his brothers after all they have done to him. They almost killed him when he was younger, and ended up selling him to slave-traders. They come to buy grain from Egypt, and eventually they realize that their long-lost brother is still alive and is now prime minister of Egypt. But how does Joseph respond? Is he looking for revenge? Has his success gone to his head and he wants nothing to do with his poor relations? No. Again and again, he states that it was God who sent him to Egypt and it was God who made him ruler of all Egypt. He doesn't harbour resentment against his brothers, because he knows God is sovereign and in control.

The second instance is when he and his celebrity wife – Asenath – start their family. Children get named all sorts of things these days. We've called our son Boaz – and that's had its fair share of comments. But Boaz isn't a patch on the creativity of Joseph and Asenath.

Joseph named his firstborn Manasseh and said, 'It is because
God has made me forget all my trouble and all my father's
household.' The second son he named Ephraim and said,
'It is because God has made me fruitful in the land of my
suffering.'
(Genesis 41:51–52)

Putting the creativity to one side, the common thread in
those two names is the four-word phrase 'God has made me'.
God has made me forget all my troubles and God has made
me fruitful in the land of my suffering, says Joseph. In both
the success and the suffering, Joseph acknowledges that
it is God who is in control. He is not boastful in success,
nor is he bitter in suffering. All because he recognizes the
sovereignty of God.

Above all, when we are on the up, we need to have *a correct
view of ourselves*. Like Joseph, we need to be clear that it is
God who has made us – he is the one in control and totally
sovereign.

The truth is that failure is being successful at the things
that don't ultimately matter.

When you are going down . . .

What about the times when things are much more difficult
at work? Down times can come very suddenly. They did for
Joseph when he was thrown into prison, and they can for
us. Today we could be making lots of money, but then
tomorrow, quick as a flash, we could be made redundant. A
collapse of the market, a takeover, a cutback, reorganization,
global recession – any one of these can change everything.
We're out of a job, we can't pay the mortgage, and we're on
the dole searching around for one of the few jobs left in our
industry.

While the key to not wilting in our faith when we are on the up is to have a correct view of ourselves, the key to not wilting in our faith when we are going down is to have *a correct view of God*.

One of the most famous promises in Scripture, that God will protect us and do what is best for us, can be found in Romans 8:28: 'And we know that in all things God works for the good of those who love him.' The apostle Paul has just been writing about struggles and sin and groaning and pain. Then he suddenly says that in all things God works for our good. Can that be true? Good in all things?

When my boss lands a heap of work on my desk and I haven't a clue how I'm going to get it all done . . . good in all things?

When I'm made redundant and I've got a family to feed . . . good in all things?

When I'm being victimized at work and it has been causing me so much stress that I have to take time off sick . . . good in all things?

When the only work I can get is a dead-end job that doesn't use any of my gifts or talents . . . good in all things?

We find it all but impossible to believe it can be true that in all things God works for the good of those who love him. In these down times, we start to despise and resent God, and that's why we need a correct view of God, which is exactly what Paul gives us after he has written Romans 8:28.

For those God foreknew he also predestined to be conformed to the likeness of his Son, that he might be the firstborn among many brothers. And those he predestined, he also called; those he called, he also justified; those he justified, he also glorified.
(Romans 8:29–30)

These two verses show us the eternal plan of God. From way before I was even a twinkle in my parents' eyes, right through to when God calls me home to be with him in glory, I am a part of his eternal plan. You are too. We have been on God's mind for a very long time. We're part of his eternal plan – a plan that will not 'separate us from the love of God that is in Christ Jesus our Lord' (Romans 8:39).

Lisa Beamer lost her husband Todd on Flight 93 on 11 September 2001, and this is what she has written:

> God knew the terrible choices the terrorists would make and that Todd would die as a result. He knew my children would be left without a father and me without a husband . . . Yet in his sovereignty and in his perspective on the big picture, he knew it was better to allow the events to unfold as they did rather than redirect Todd's plans to avoid death . . . I can't see all the reasons he might have allowed this when I know he could have stopped it . . . I don't know God's plan, and honestly, right now I don't like it very much. But I trust that he is true to his promise in Romans 8:28: 'We know that in all things God works for the good of those who love him.' My only responsibility is to love God. He'll work out the rest.[2]

Whatever down situations take place in our lives and in our work, Lisa Beamer's challenge is our challenge too. We are to have a correct view of God. We are to hold on to the truth that God works for our good, even if we can't fully understand it in the here and now.

The secret of contentment

> I have learned to be content whatever the circumstances. I know what it is to be in need, and I know what it is to have

plenty. I have learned the secret of being content in any and every situation, whether well fed or hungry, whether living in plenty or in want.
(Philippians 4:11–12)

In the ups and downs of Paul's life, he had learned to be content whatever the circumstances. Partly, the secret of his contentment would have been having a correct view of himself when he was on the up, and a correct view of God when he was experiencing a down time. But as you read the whole of Paul's letter to the Philippians, it seems that he didn't just have a correct view of himself and God. The secret to his contentment was also that he looked both backwards and forwards.

He looked backwards at his past – at both the successes and the failures – and he said, 'I consider everything a loss compared to the surpassing greatness of knowing Christ Jesus my Lord' (Philippians 3:8). He considered everything rubbish compared to knowing forgiveness for sin through faith in Christ's death on the cross. He also looked forwards to the future and knew that, while it would have its ups and downs, his long-term future was amazing. He said, 'Our citizenship is in heaven. And we eagerly await a Saviour from there, the Lord Jesus Christ, who, by the power that enables him to bring everything under his control, will transform our lowly bodies so that they will be like his glorious body' (Philippians 3:20–21). As Paul looks to the future, he speaks of the biggest 'up time' of all.

It's the same for us. In both the ups and the downs of work, like Paul, we need to look backwards and forwards, rather than just focusing on our current circumstances in the here and now.

So look backwards through the good times and the bad times, and through your sins, your failures and your regrets.

Look back until you come in your mind's eye all the way back to the cross, and believe that all your sin has been paid for there by Jesus. Every last bit. You have been provided with *God's amazing forgiveness*. As a believer, sin can spoil your relationship with God, but it cannot separate you from him. You need to let this amazing forgiveness mould and influence your daily living. When all is well at work, it will ensure that you don't get too puffed up. After all, the only thing that you contribute to your forgiveness is your sin – the very thing for which you need to be forgiven. And when all is down at work, the cross will ensure that you don't get pulled too far down. You won't get eaten up by your regrets and failures because you'll remember you are totally forgiven. Forgiven, because on the cross Christ was forsaken.

And look forwards. Through the potential ups and downs, through the things you are excited about and the things you dread. Look forwards to the decisions you have to make and to the things that seem uncertain at the moment. Look forwards even to death itself, and then keep looking forwards until you come in your mind's eye all the way to heaven. If you are in Christ, then heaven is *your amazing future*. Whatever is happening in life, whether you are in an up or down time at the moment, this is a reminder that the future is far better. Looking at your present situation with heaven's eternal perspective will be a comfort in the down times so that you don't get too pulled down, and a correction in the up times so that you don't get too puffed up.

Looking back to God's amazing forgiveness; looking forwards to our amazing future. That is the secret of contentment. That is the secret to not wilting in our faith as we keep on bouncing up and down throughout our working life.

Recap

5. Surviving the ups and downs

When you are on the up ... Have a correct view of yourself
- Ready to shine for God
- Refuse to sin against God
- Recognize the sovereignty of God

When you are going down ... Have a correct view of God
'In all things God works for the good of those who love him'

The secret of contentment
- Look backwards ➡ God's amazing forgiveness
- Look forwards ➡ Your amazing future

Relate

Name: Andy Stewart
Occupation: Freelance computer programmer

Work has its ups and downs like any other area of life. Everyone takes a different path and has their own set of experiences, but for me two areas have proved troublesome.

The first is work swamping the rest of my life. Like many people, I try to be conscientious and not let others down. However, over time many companies begin to take their employees' good will for granted and demand more and more. Some add hypocrisy to the mix by regularly expecting people to stay several hours late, but then outlawing a few minutes of personal e-mail during the day.

One project I worked on had the team staying until 10pm most evenings, and working weekends. For several months I barely saw my wife, let alone my friends. I believe God wants us to work hard, but not at the expense of the other things he has for us to do – like being there for our family and friends. This was the third such project, and crossed the line I had drawn in my mind (my mind is one big sandy beach). So I completed the project to the best of my ability, and then resigned a few months later.

My second struggle has been with the two bosses for whom I lost all respect. All my other bosses were excellent, and I am grateful to have worked for them. In contrast I felt my two nemeses had reached their positions through ethically dubious means, and treated their staff carelessly.

At the time I decided that to keep my integrity, and not be two-faced, I shouldn't hide my feelings. Instead, if they asked for my opinion, I would say exactly what I thought. This policy led to a number of uncomfortable meetings, and more flack for me.

Looking back, I wonder what my nemeses thought of Jesus when dealing with my borderline insubordination. I could perhaps have been more tactful without compromising my integrity. I should probably have tried to love them, despite their flaws. Certainly I should have prayed for them more.

Moving to the ups of work, I believe it's crucial to define your own success. Don't thoughtlessly accept other people's definition of success (goals achieved, pay rises, promotions, etc.); those are out of your control and set you up for distress. Instead define your success by God's criteria: to love him with all your heart, soul, strength and mind, and to love your neighbour as yourself.

This has the useful side-effect of making your regular appraisals less stressful. If your boss fails to give you the recognition you deserve, but you have defined your success by other criteria, then it's nothing to worry about.

There's a Jewish tradition of carrying around a small piece of card which says, on one side, 'You are a sinner,' and on the other, 'You are precious to God.' When you're feeling smug you look at the first side, and when you're feeling low you look at the other. Simple and effective!

Respond

1. Do you feel ready for all the ups and downs of the workplace?
2. What are the biggest challenges to your faith when all is going well at work? And what are the biggest challenges when things are going badly?
3. Paul writes, 'I have learned to be content whatever the circumstances.' Can you echo his sentiments? If not, why not?

PART 3

WORK LIKE A TROUT

*How to display Christ-like attitudes and actions
at work*

When you have two small children, weekend lie-ins suddenly become a thing of the past – unless you dump the children with their grandparents. The first time my wife Susannah and I managed to do this was a much anticipated event. We had booked the weekend a year in advance, and it was a wonderful time in a hotel in the Brecon Beacons in Wales – full of enormous lie-ins that would have impressed any teenager. But when we did get up, one of the main attractions of where we were staying was that there was an opportunity to fly-fish for trout on the river just below the hotel.

If you've never gone fly-fishing, you should. As far as I can tell, all other types of fishing require zero skill. You just plonk your line in the water and wait and see if you get lucky and a fish decides to come and gobble up whatever tasty morsel you have on the end of your line. Fly-fishing is very different. You're fishing on a river, looking for where a trout rises to the surface to eat a fly on the water. And when you spot a rise, then you have to cast your line so that the fly on the end of your line lands a few yards upstream of the fish. It's a huge skill. You have to make sure you don't get the line caught in the branches hanging over the river. You have to make sure the fishing line lands delicately on the surface of the water so it doesn't scare the fish. And then you wait with baited breath (excuse the pun) while the flow of the river takes your line downstream, dragging your fly over the unsuspecting trout. Fly-fishing is a hugely skilful sport. I would go as far as to say it is an art form. My grandpa first taught me to fly-fish when I was about six years old. I consider myself something of an expert.

So it was somewhat galling when my wife turned to me in the middle of our kid-free weekend and announced, 'In all the nine years I have known you, you have never caught a trout.' Harsh – but true.

As I have reflected over many unsuccessful hours standing in rivers, with many trout enjoying being near such an incompetent fisherman, it has struck me that the trout is a good picture of the Christian at work. This is for one simple reason: the trout always faces upstream and swims against the flow of the river.

As Christians in the workplace, there are times when we are going to need to go against the flow – that is, against the general flow of the culture of a workplace where the majority of individuals do not have a relationship with Jesus. Of course, the way others operate at work will often be totally in line with how we feel Jesus wants us to operate. But there is no denying that there will be times when there is a tension, and it is at those times that the Christian should look to go against the flow.

Jesus' Sermon on the Mount, recorded in Matthew 5 – 7, is perhaps the most well known of all his teachings and it is all about Christians going against the flow. In summarizing the Sermon on the Mount, John Stott says, 'It is the nearest thing to a manifesto that [Jesus] ever uttered, for it is his own description of what he wanted his followers to be and do. To my mind no two words sum up its intention better, or indicate more clearly its challenge to the modern world, than the expression "Christian counter-culture".'[1] That's why, in Part 3 of this book, it is Jesus' teaching in the Sermon on the Mount that will form the frame that helps us think through how to live out a truly Christian counter-culture in our workplaces.

Make no mistake. This is vitally important. We will wilt in our faith if we aren't counter-cultural. As the evangelist J. John quips, 'It's only dead fish that go with the flow.'[2]

6. AGAINST THE FLOW CHARACTER

Blessed are the poor in spirit,
    for theirs is the kingdom of heaven.
Blessed are those who mourn,
    for they will be comforted.
Blessed are the meek,
    for they will inherit the earth.
Blessed are those who hunger and thirst for righteousness,
    for they will be filled.
Blessed are the merciful,
    for they will be shown mercy.
Blessed are the pure in heart,
    for they will see God.
Blessed are the peacemakers,
    for they will be called sons of God.
Blessed are those who are persecuted because of
      righteousness,
    for theirs is the kingdom of heaven.
Blessed are you when people insult you, persecute you and
falsely say all kinds of evil against you because of me. Rejoice
and be glad, because great is your reward in heaven, for in the
same way they persecuted the prophets who were before you.
(Matthew 5:3–12)

In 2006, the Queen celebrated her eightieth birthday. As is
usual on these occasions, she sat for a portrait, which strikes
me as a rather dull way of celebrating your birthday, but there
you go. However, I guess the sitting for the painting must
have been livened up a bit for the Queen because the person
commissioned to paint her portrait was the Australian

cartoonist and musician Rolf Harris, who never seems at a loss for words.

In fact, there was quite a lot of surprise, not only about Rolf Harris being chosen as the artist, but also about the portrait he painted. In the painting the Queen wasn't wearing any crown or huge jewels or amazing ball gown as would have been expected. She was just sitting in a fairly ordinary chair in a fairly ordinary green outfit. When asked about his painting, Rolf Harris commented that he 'wanted to capture the lady as she is with all her humour and reality' – which I'm guessing the Queen would have been quite flattered by. I just hope she didn't hear his next comment on the painting: 'I really like the way you get the blueness of the veins coming through the skin.' A fine example of Australian tact.

I wonder if the surprise at the Queen's portrait is also mirrored in our surprise as we look at the portrait Jesus paints of a Christian at the start of the Sermon on the Mount. Blessed are those who are poor in spirit, who mourn, who are meek, who are merciful, who are pure in heart, who are persecuted. This is not exactly an obvious skill-set to highlight on our CV, is it?

If we tell people at work that it's better to be poor than rich (v. 3) – whether materially or spiritually – people will think we're loopy. If we tell colleagues that it's good to mourn (v. 4), or to be meek (v. 5), then they will think we've lost it. And if we tell them how good it is to be persecuted and insulted (vv. 10–12), then they will probably sign us off for sick leave and think we're nuts. Jesus encourages us to have a character that very much goes against the flow.

A portrait of a Christian at work

So what might it actually look like to live out the Beatitudes at work? Dream a little . . .

We'll be people who acknowledge that we are spiritually bankrupt before God and have nothing to commend ourselves to him – poor in spirit. We'll be upset when we have treated our colleagues badly or let them down. We won't be self-righteous at work, thinking that we're pretty good and moral. We won't be a bit of a wet blanket – but we will be humble. We won't see the need to do everything to protect our own interests and make sure we look good and are well thought of. We won't be ambitious, aggressive, or cut-throat in trying to get to the top. Because actually we'll know that we're going to have everything in the future – we're going to inherit the earth – so what we have now is of relatively little importance.

While others might be hungering and thirsting for more money, more status, or more sexual fulfilment, we'll be thirsting for righteousness. We'll be people who say, 'I'm sorry.' We'll be people who say, 'I forgive you.' We'll be people who know we make mistakes, so admit them, and are understanding when others make mistakes as well. We'll be utterly sincere and totally transparent in our dealings with people. We'll be authentic – our actions will match our thoughts, our character on a Sunday will match our character on a Monday. We'll long for peace for our colleagues – horizontally between them when there are tensions, and vertically when there is tension between them and God. We will want peace and we will actually look to make it happen.

. . . time to wake up now.

It's quite a dream, isn't it? If you've spent any time at all in a workplace, you'll know how difficult it is to live out the kind of character that Jesus paints for us. Our natural reaction is that if we even manage something approaching that kind of counter-cultural character at work, then surely all our colleagues will think we're the most amazingly generous and kind-hearted individuals and will be asking us, 'What must I do to be saved?' before the week is out.

That's not quite the case, though. Jesus' portrait of the Christian also includes mention of persecution. In fact, of all the Beatitudes, the one that starts, 'Blessed are those who are persecuted . . . ' is the only one that is expanded by Jesus for another two verses. Let's be clear. You can be persecuted by your colleagues at work for being an awkward so-and-so who's really difficult to work with, or you can be persecuted by your colleagues for your taste in revolting ties with cartoon characters on them. But that's not what Jesus is talking about here. Jesus says, 'Blessed are you when people insult you, persecute you and falsely say all kinds of evil against you *because of me.*' Even if we are living out this amazing Christ-defined character in our workplace, it's likely that we will be persecuted because of our connection to Jesus.

This is the portrait of a Christian according to Jesus. And if you're anything like me, that brings you up short. So often the Beatitudes are thought to be not Beatitudes, but platitudes. They're seen as prime fodder for those greetings cards or posters you can get in Christian bookshops – a picture of a cat playing with a ball of wool, and beneath it a nice little Beatitude. 'Greetings card' Christianity is not what Jesus is talking about here. 'Blood, sweat and tears' Christianity would be a more accurate and honest description.[1] This is a tough ask from Jesus.

The influence of a Christian at work

It may be tough to have this 'against the flow' character. We have seen that it is quite possible that it will result in us being persecuted at work. Yet that does not mean we will have no influence at all. Jesus makes it very clear what the influence of the Christian in the workplace can be. As Jesus continues the Sermon on the Mount, that is exactly what he is talking about – how you and I can be an influence for good in our workplace.

> You are the salt of the earth. But if the salt loses its saltiness, how can it be made salty again? It is no longer good for anything, except to be thrown out and trampled by men.
>
> You are the light of the world. A city on a hill cannot be hidden. Neither do people light a lamp and put it under a bowl. Instead they put it on its stand, and it gives light to everyone in the house. In the same way, let your light shine before men, that they may see your good deeds and praise your Father in heaven.
>
> (Matthew 5:13–16)

You are the salt of the earth

Jesus says that if salt loses its saltiness, it is useless – presumably because then it's just like everything else around it. So this is his call to us to be *distinct* – that's what we need to be if we are going to be a positive influence in our workplaces, because our danger is that we conform to the surroundings in which we find ourselves.

A young police officer was taking his final exam. One of his questions went like this: 'You are on patrol in outer London when an explosion occurs in a gas main in a nearby street. On investigation you find that a large hole has been blown in the footpath and there is an overturned van nearby. Inside the van there is a strong smell of alcohol. Both occupants – a man and a woman – are injured. You recognize the woman as the wife of your Divisional Inspector, who is at present away in the USA. A passing motorist stops to offer you assistance and you realize that he is a man wanted for armed robbery. Suddenly a man runs out of a nearby house, shouting that his wife is expecting a baby and the explosion has made the birth imminent. Another man is crying for help, having been blown into the adjacent canal by the explosion, and he cannot swim. Describe in a few words what you would do.'

The police officer thought for a moment before writing his answer to the question: 'I would take off my uniform and mingle with the crowd.'[2]

We can sympathize with his actions. The urge to be part of the crowd and not be distinct is a strong one because it is so much easier and less of a challenge. But Jesus is calling us to be as distinct as a uniformed police officer is in a crowd of civilians. We are to be distinct by living out the Beatitudes in our attitudes and our actions.

You are the light of the world

Being the light of the world is not so much about being distinct as being *radiant*. It's about us shining brightly for our Father in heaven with whoever or whatever comes into contact with us. That's also how to have a positive influence at work. And while the danger with salt for the Christian is the danger of conforming, the danger with light is the danger of concealing. Jesus says we should not put our light under a bowl. Don't conceal it.

Yet sometimes we do conceal the light *physically* by removing ourselves from people who aren't yet Christians. So Nicky Gumbel, the vicar of Holy Trinity Brompton, comments that 'Christians need to be salt and light in their work environments. That is why we should not give up working in a secular environment unless we are specifically called out of it. We are called to have an influence in the office, factory, police force, hospital, shop, or wherever it is that we are working. This is where front line ministry takes place.'[3]

I think of an e-mail I got from someone who was a final-year student, who was debating what type of job to go into and was considering being a management consultant. 'I'm finding it hard to justify working in something that seems so unrelated to God's purposes,' she wrote. Her problem was that she didn't have Jesus' perspective on work. Jesus would encourage her to be the light of the world. Unless she felt that God particularly wanted her to serve in a Christian organization, management consultancy would be a perfectly reasonable job to have that is very much related to God's purposes. In that job she could be a light to that world.

Sometimes we conceal our light *morally*. When Jesus speaks about us being a light, first and foremost he is thinking not about our verbal witness to Christ, but about our good deeds (v. 16). So often, however, our good deeds evaporate in the dog-eat-dog world of the workplace. We let the culture of our workplace transform us, when Christ longs to use us to transform our workplace.

Ann is a Christian nurse. While on her shift on the ward, she went missing for two hours. No-one could find her anywhere, until someone opened a cupboard and found Ann hidden there reading her Bible, when she was supposed to be going about her duties on the ward. Ann was being irresponsible on many levels. She was morally concealing the light and as a result was not having a positive influence among her colleagues.

We also conceal our light *verbally*. Even if we are interacting with our colleagues and spending time with them, even if we do act in an upright way, there is still concealment because we are never upfront about our connection to Jesus Christ. We never speak of him – this person who in church we affirm as the most important person in our life. If we never speak about Jesus, then verse 16 cannot completely take place: 'In the same way, let your light shine before men, that they

may see your good deeds and praise your Father in heaven.'
If we don't speak about Jesus, our colleagues will see our
good deeds, but they will never praise our Father in heaven.
Without the verbal dimension, our colleagues will praise us
rather than our Father. They will just say how thoughtful,
calm and nice we are. They won't praise God.

It is a challenge to be an influence for Christ at work. It
is why we need to ask God to be working in us more and
more by his Spirit, to have this 'against the flow' character.

And yet with this challenge, please be encouraged too.
Throughout your working life, as you step into your workplace each day, remember that you are in a huge position of
influence for Christ. You can directly influence far more
people, day in day out, than someone like me who spends
his time surrounded by lots of other Christians. As you go
into your workplace each day, remind yourself: 'I am to be
salt here, I am to be light here.' And then ask God to mould
your 'against the flow' character and help you to be faithful
in that role.

Recap

6. Against the flow character

A portrait of a Christian at work
  ⮕ Beatitudes, not platitudes

The influence of a Christian at work
You are the salt of the earth   ⮕ Be distinct. Don't conform
You are the light of the world   ⮕ Be radiant. Don't conceal

Relate

Name: Katharine Dryer
Occupation: Director, global investment management
company

'Have you ever thought of going into banking?' Bombarded by rejection letters, I was beginning to wonder if I would ever move on from this mundane temping job. I snapped back, 'No. I can't count!' Eight interviews and a maths test later, here I was. I knew that God had put me here. However, having spent four years wafting around Oxford reading Medieval German poetry, striding into an investment management house in two-inch heels felt like entering a different world.

The job kicked off with a two-month residential course for all the bank's trainee fund managers, traders and investment bankers. It was full-on and it was fast. Ambition, greed, drink and testosterone made the world turn. The office environment was less intense, but the arrogance and competition were just as fierce. Success was so often achieved by putting others down. Standing out as a Christian was not difficult – I stuck out like a sore thumb. The challenge lay in building relationships with people, succeeding in the job and yet remaining true to my faith.

I really had no idea how challenging that first year at work would be. It pushed me to the limit intellectually and emotionally. I allowed my identity to become very wrapped up in the job and as a result, my confidence crumbled. I was 'pond life' in the office and something of a misfit after hours. The recurring question in my mind was, 'God, what am I doing here?' I found it so hard to trust in God's sovereignty and believe that I could survive in the City by doing things his way.

As I've progressed in my career, the challenges have changed a bit. Somehow it has been easier to bring more of myself to the job as my professional skills have developed. However, the politics and power plays become more acute. It's still hard to find the balance between managing your profile upwards yet finding time for everyone, being assertive and delivering under pressure yet being gentle to all, enjoying success yet taming selfish ambition. Although I have often doubted his plan, God has always walked with me and taught me. When the pressures have become too great, he has intervened to provide a way forward.

Every few months I play squash with an old MBA friend. It's a familiar routine: I flail around the court, he wins without breaking sweat and then we go for a beer. One evening I caught him in philosophical mood: 'It's incredible to me that you do your job, you know how the City works and yet you still hold on to your Christian faith – I don't know how your beliefs don't get swallowed up by everything around you.' People don't get it. Apart from the grace of God, it doesn't make sense. But if, in a few better moments, I can make people stop and think, be the discomforting exception to the rule, point to a bigger picture . . . that's a project worth running with.

Respond

1. How would your colleagues or future colleagues react if you lived out the Beatitudes at work?

2. At work, Jesus wants us to be distinct and not conform. And he wants us to be radiant and not conceal. How do you need to change to have a greater influence for Jesus at work?

3. At work you are in a huge position of influence for Christ. How does that make you feel?

7. AGAINST THE FLOW RELATIONSHIPS

One of the most successful TV comedy series of the twenty-first century has been *The Office*, written by Ricky Gervais and Stephen Merchant, and starring Ricky Gervais. It was *The Office* that catapulted Gervais to stardom in 2001. He won two Golden Globes, one for his acting and one for the show itself. If you've never watched it, *The Office* was basically filmed as 'a fly-on-the-wall documentary about modern office life'. It is, of course, a fictional comedy documentary – a 'mocumentary' is the technical term. The humour is very simple. It comes from observations about mundane office life, humour basically at the expense of all the different types of people working in the office. In fact, just as the TV series *Friends* was called *Friends* because it was about the relationships between different friends, so *The Office* could just as easily have been called *Colleagues*, because it's all about the relationships between different colleagues.

You've got Tim, the sales rep, who is the 'dissatisfied with life' colleague played by Martin Freeman. He's a nice guy, but at thirty, he still lives with his parents and works in a job he believes to be completely pointless. You've got the 'frustrating' colleague, Gareth, who gets on everyone's nerves. Gareth is a humourless jobsworth. You've got the 'attractive' colleague, Dawn, the receptionist. Tim fancies her, but she's engaged to someone else. And then you've got the 'nightmare' colleague, the boss, David Brent, played by Ricky Gervais. David Brent thinks he's friendly, hilarious and well liked, but the reality is very different.

Much of the success of the programme comes about because, if we have been in the workplace for any time at all, we can all relate to people in our own workplaces who are like each one of the characters. Probably even now you're thinking of someone you know who is just like Gareth . . .

The Sermon on the Mount obviously came out a few years before *The Office*. And Jesus' teaching in the sermon is, thankfully, very different in style and content from David Brent's. Yet Jesus' teaching still helps us to think about how we relate to all the different types of colleagues we get to observe in *The Office* – in a way that is very much against the flow of the culture of most workplaces.

Relating to frustrating colleagues (like Gareth)

Colleagues can be frustrating for a whole number of reasons, can't they? I can think of one person who used to work for me who had zero attention to detail. She made the same mistakes again and again. Then there was the person I worked for who was appalling at delegation. Everything had to go through him. No-one was able to make any decisions without him. As a result we always missed our deadlines because we were awaiting his approval on any bit of work we did. You won't need to be in the workplace long before you meet some frustrating colleagues, and when you do, the temptation is to get angry with them, or bitter in your heart.

> You have heard that it was said to the people long ago, 'Do not murder, and anyone who murders will be subject to judgment.' But I tell you that anyone who is angry with his brother will be subject to judgment.
> (Matthew 5:21–22)

There will be very few people reading this book who have committed murder, and yet Jesus doesn't let us off the hook. Because we have all been angry, we've committed murder in our hearts and so Jesus goes on to tell us how we should act towards that person with whom we're angry.

> Therefore, if you are offering your gift at the altar and there remember that your brother has something against you, leave your gift there in front of the altar. First go and be reconciled to your brother; then come and offer your gift.
> Settle matters quickly with your adversary.
> (Matthew 5:23–25)

Jesus tells us to deal with our anger at once. It's wise advice, because we all know from painful experience that if we leave anger unchecked for a while, if we allow it to brew in us, it can quickly reach devastating levels and cause untold disaster. Don't let it grow, says Jesus. He says that we need *quick reconciliation rather than growing anger*. We who are Christians in our workplace are the ones who need to take the initiative in being reconciled with our colleagues. Even our frustrating ones.

In any marriage preparation course, there's always a bit about how the most important phrases to learn in marriage are 'I'm sorry' and 'Please forgive me'. That's wise advice for marriage, but actually those are words that we need to learn just as much in the workplace. This is hugely counter-cultural. It's against the flow of the workplace culture. People very rarely say 'I'm sorry' at work. Rather, they look to make excuses, or blame others, or somehow rationalize what they've done. People do anything to avoid saying 'I'm sorry'. They don't want to be seen to be weak or ruin their career prospects.

As Christians, we should be different. We should be just as ready to say 'sorry' when we make a mistake at work as in any other area of life. 'I'm sorry. I forgot to phone the client.' Or perhaps, 'I'm sorry for just blowing my fuse and flying off the handle.' But at other times, it's our colleagues who should be saying 'sorry' – and yet they don't. They may be the ones who are highly frustrating, but Jesus is telling us in the Sermon on the Mount that it is we, as Christians, who need to take the initiative to be reconciled.

Take Chris, who works for one of the main London radio stations. Chris was really disheartened by the way his boss was constantly giving him and another colleague lots of work to do when other people in the department had very little to do and were leaving work early. It seemed so unfair. Understandably, Chris was frustrated and so he asked to meet me after work one day to discuss what he should do in the situation. As we chatted over a beer, we even went as far as roughly scripting what he would say to his boss so that his words were as gracious as they could be, while being honest about why he was hurt. Just before we finished talking, I asked Chris when he planned to have this conversation with his boss. I was quite surprised by his response. He may not have been very definite about what to say to his boss, but he was crystal clear on when he should have the conversation. This is what he said: 'Tomorrow morning. If I leave it longer, then I'll say it all angrily in the heat of the moment when I'm really cross about something, and I don't want to do that.'

As I walked away from the pub that evening and thought about my chat with Chris, I realized that what he had said was in total agreement with Jesus' teaching in the Sermon on the Mount. Quick reconciliation is far better than growing anger – even towards frustrating colleagues like Chris's boss.

Relating to attractive colleagues (like Dawn, or the male equivalent)

Frustrating colleagues may be one thing, but a rather different, though equally challenging proposition is how we relate to those colleagues whom we find really attractive.

I can remember one evening when I had just started as a management consultant. I was on a training course with about twenty other recent graduates in a four-star hotel in Surrey. I had never seen anything like my room in the hotel – the bed was so big it was wider than it was long. One night during the course, everyone was in the hotel bar and the drinks were flowing, helped by the fact that it was all free. Good little Christian boy that I was, I decided to head back to my room at about 11pm so that before hitting the sack, I could have a quick time with God praying and reading my Bible – which I had failed to do so far that day.

So there I was – an angelic picture, in my pyjamas, in bed, reading my Bible.

Suddenly there comes a knock on the door. It opens, and in walks – or rather stumbles – an extremely attractive colleague. Tall, slim, blonde, bubbly personality. She sprawls herself across my bed – the one that is wider than it is long. And there I am, in my pyjamas, reading my Bible.

The workplace is full of sexual temptation. I thank God that he helped me resist doing anything stupid that night. But we need to be aware of the dangers. The workplace is an affair incubator. According to a recent survey, 48% of workers have known a married colleague to have an affair with some-one else in their workplace.[1]

Some of us will have failed in what Jesus says in Matthew 5:27 as he continues the Sermon on the Mount: 'You have heard that it was said, "Do not commit adultery."' But even if we haven't, Jesus doesn't let us feel smug and superior, because all of us will have fallen at the very next hurdle: 'But I tell you that anyone who looks at a woman lustfully has already committed adultery with her in his heart' (Matthew 5:28).

We need to be clear what is and what is not 'looking lust-fully' at someone. It's not looking lustfully to look at them and think, 'You're attractive.' But it is looking lustfully to think, 'You're attractive and I want to dwell on what you look like quite a bit more for my own personal titillation.' It's also looking lustfully if you think, 'You're attractive and I want you to find me attractive too,' if that person is not someone you could seriously consider as a potential marriage partner – because (a) they are married, (b) you are married, or (c) that person is not a Christian. All of us have to be honest and admit that, even if we haven't failed the verse 27 test, we have failed the verse 28 test. Looking lustfully is committing heart adultery.

This does run the risk of you thinking I'm a dirty old man, but let me give you three examples of how I've committed heart adultery at work.

Number 1: walking a certain route from my desk when I go to the water cooler for a drink so that I always pass by and am able to have a look at the person I think is very attractive.

Number 2: I'm single and at the office Christmas party. I've been sitting next to a colleague who obviously rather likes me; in fact, she had something to do with the seating arrangement. I think she's attractive. She's not a Christian. At the end of the meal there's salsa dancing. She asks me to dance with her. I agree. I've certainly got lustful thoughts going on as I dance with her.

Number 3: on the London Underground on the way to work each day, I find myself being most interested in staring at the woman in the same carriage as me whom I find most attractive.

As Jesus performs his heart scan on us, it becomes clear that we've all committed heart adultery. That is why Jesus' message to all of us is that relating to attractive colleagues at work requires *radical decisions rather than casual lust.*

> If your right eye causes you to sin, gouge it out and throw it away. It is better for you to lose one part of your body than for your whole body to be thrown into hell. And if your right hand causes you to sin, cut it off and throw it away. It is better for you to lose one part of your body than for your whole body to go into hell.
>
> (Matthew 5:29–30)

Of course, Jesus doesn't mean a literal, physical self-maiming. After all, if I gouge my right eye out, I can still commit heart adultery with my left. But he does mean that we should take radical steps so that we deal drastically with being tempted to lust – rather than just flirting with it. Jesus says we must take control of our eyes (v. 29). In other words, we should take care over what we look at: the glances on the train, the internet sites. He says we must take control of our hands too (v. 30). In other words, we should take care over what we do. So if we're attracted to a colleague who is 'off limits' for whatever reason, we must make sure that we don't spend prolonged time with that person. We should organize it so that where possible it's not just the two of us travelling together, or just the two of us having a meeting together. And we should make sure that in no way do we start having a relationship that is in any way 'special' or 'exclusive' – in terms of our conversations, our e-mails or our lunchbreaks.

Remember Joseph with his boss's wife? As she tried to seduce him and drag him into bed with her, how did Joseph respond to what must have been an attractive and flattering offer? How would you have responded?

'No thank you, I won't have sex with you because that would be wrong. But would you like to come and have a coffee with me at Starbucks, because there's nothing wrong with that? And then maybe we could go to a movie afterwards, because again there's nothing wrong with that either.' That's not how Joseph responded, is it?

Joseph didn't flirt with casual lust. He fled from it and from her. The account says that he refused even to spend time with her (Genesis 39:10). In Joseph's workplace, as in the rest of life, he knew there had to be radical decisions rather than casual lust. Without wanting to sound too much like a drama queen, radical decision-making is required because this heart problem is deadly. Jesus says that failure to take this seriously means we're in danger of hell. It's shocking talk. He is speaking here to those who claim to be his disciples, and yet he says that sexual sin can lead us down a path to somewhere where there is actually no connection to him at all.

Relating to nightmare colleagues (like David Brent)

'If you've ever secretly harboured thoughts that a colleague – or even your boss – behaves like a psychopath, you may be closer to the truth than you dared imagine.' That was the first line in a recent article in the *Guardian* entitled 'Beware – danger at work'. The article went on to quote Professor Hare of the University of British Columbia in Canada.

> Corporate psychopaths tend to be manipulative, arrogant, callous, impatient, impulsive, unreliable and prone to fly into rages. They break promises and take credit for the work of others and blame everyone else when things go wrong. Psychopaths are social predators and like all predators they look for feeding grounds. Wherever you get power, prestige and money you will find them.[2]

It doesn't take long at work before one of these delightful individuals turns up. It could be someone at the same level as you, or, as in the case of *The Office*, it could be your boss.

The question is, how should the Christian go about relating to the nightmare that is the corporate psychopath? I looked on a website about office politics, and one person had the following suggestion: 'After repeated torrents of verbal abuse, I have to confess to on two occasions, putting laxative in my manager's tea.'[3]

Jesus' teaching is a little different.

> You have heard that it was said, 'Eye for eye, and tooth for tooth.' But I tell you, Do not resist an evil person. If someone strikes you on the right cheek, turn to him the other also.
> (Matthew 5:38–39)

> You have heard that it was said, 'Love your neighbour and hate your enemy.' But I tell you: Love your enemies and pray for those who persecute you.'
> (Matthew 5:43–44)

Jesus suggests that we should relate to nightmare colleagues with *practical love rather than rightful revenge*. This call to show love is for two reasons. First, Jesus says that it marks us as *in* God's family. A mark of being connected to our Father in heaven is that we love our enemies (Matthew 5:45). Second, it marks us *out* from the world around us. Jesus continues, 'If you love those who love you, what reward will you get? Are not even the tax collectors doing that? And if you greet only your brothers, what are you doing more than others? Do not even pagans do that?' (Matthew 5:46–47) We need to be radically different from our colleagues.

So don't gang up on the nightmare person at work, as so often happens. Rather, love them and include them. Maybe pray for the nightmare boss, or buy a coffee for the nightmare colleague. Caroline had a nightmare colleague, called Sonia.

Caroline would often be blamed by Sonia for all the mistakes that Sonia made. It was very hurtful and made the office a very difficult place to be. But as a Christian, Caroline knew she needed to try to love Sonia. She offered to stay late to help Sonia with the work she was behind on, and when she couldn't help in that way, she left notes of encouragement on Sonia's desk to show her that she cared about her. It was incredibly difficult to do, when Caroline really wanted to get revenge for all the hurt Sonia had caused her. But looking back, Caroline is so glad that the Lord gave her the strength to show practical love, and she can see how that love was the platform that provided opportunities to share the message of the gospel with Sonia.

Dissatisfied as a colleague (like Tim)?

> Be perfect, therefore, as your heavenly Father is perfect.
> (Matthew 5:48)

Throughout this chapter, as we have thought about how we relate to the different types of colleagues we have or will have, I wonder how you have felt. Have you felt satisfied or dissatisfied? If you're anything like me, more often than not with the frustrating colleague you show growing anger rather than quick reconciliation. More often than not with the attractive colleague you show casual lust rather than radical decisions. More often than not with the nightmare colleague you show rightful revenge rather than practical love. Again and again, our relationships at work are going completely with the flow of the workplace culture.

We may want to imitate our perfect Father who shows perfect love to all, but if we're honest, that isn't what we're all like all of the time. In a way, it's right that we feel dissatisfied with ourselves. In fact, I think that's what Jesus is wanting us to realize in this section of his Sermon. Again and again, six times in twenty-seven verses, Jesus takes his listeners then, and us, his listeners now, on a journey. It's not a long journey, but it is a painful one. It's a journey into our hearts. Again and again, Jesus uses the same phrase: 'You have heard that it was said . . . but I tell you . . . ' And whether it's about murder or adultery, whether it's about our words or our actions, each time Jesus uses that phrase to take us away from the external legalistic law and on a journey through our body to our hearts.

When we see our hearts, and all that's in them, we realize how foolish we often are to be confident in our standing before God based on our own performance. We may not have murdered, but we have all committed murder in our hearts. We may not have committed adultery, but we have all committed adultery in our hearts. Jesus' words are very humbling. We can't look at others in our workplaces and say how dreadful they are compared to us. We're all in the dock before God.

As we're left feeling helpless before God, however, there is some amazingly good news. As we grieve at how we have related wrongly to colleagues, we can take comfort in how Jesus starts his whole Sermon – with the first two Beatitudes.

> Blessed are the poor in spirit,
>   for theirs is the kingdom of heaven.
> Blessed are those who mourn,
>   for they will be comforted.
> (Matthew 5:3–4)

As we go to God acknowledging that we are poor in spirit, he restores us and says that we're part of his kingdom. As we mourn at our sin, particularly at how we have treated our colleagues wrongly, God comforts us with the comfort of the gospel: the amazing comfort that Jesus died for us and took our penalty on himself so that despite our wrongdoings and imperfection we can be in a right relationship with a perfect God.

We can know comfort when we relate to God through Jesus' performance, not our own performance. Jesus' performance satisfies us, even if our own performance is dissatisfying. And that comfort is the spur to want, 'by the power of God's Spirit at work in us', to relate to all our colleagues in ways that are against the flow of the workplace culture. Against the flow – but pleasing to our Father in heaven.

Recap

7. Against the flow relationships

Relating to frustrating colleagues
Quick reconciliation rather than *growing anger*

Relating to attractive colleagues
Radical decisions rather than *casual lust*

Relating to nightmare colleagues
Practical love rather than *rightful revenge*

 Dissatisfied as a colleague?

Relate

Name: Odette Forse
Occupation: Administrator

When I first came to work in my current job, I was struck by the different array of people. Some have gone on to be good friends, but more often than not I find myself working alongside difficult personalities from all walks of life. It is a shock when you realize that these are the people with whom you spend most of your time, who see more of you than your family or close friends.

The office is a microcosm of the larger world and at times can seem incredibly intense, especially for the Christian. I think that my faith has really helped me to be much more understanding of the needs of my work colleagues and to try to be as supportive to them as possible. I have to confess that this is not always easy. The hardest thing for me is dealing with people who have strong personalities and to whom everyone else seems to have taken a dislike. There is always the usual talking in corners about certain people or the boss and sometimes you find yourself drawn into something without realizing it. I have to stand back when I see this is happening and try to remain the voice of calm, but I have to say this can be difficult.

The organization I work for is very male dominated and this too can create problems that a naive person like me just never saw coming. I guess it is part of the Christian nature to be friendly and encouraging to people, but the office can be a hotbed of romance and just because you are a Christian doesn't make you immune to the attentions of others. It took me a while to realize that this was what was happening to me. Unfortunately, telling someone that you are a Christian and not interested can make them keener and having to see that same person day in and day out can make for a bumpy ride. Being prepared that attention from work colleagues can be a reality can only be helpful, and it is not a good idea to spend too much time alone with them.

Work is a real challenge for me as a fairly new Christian. I think it is good to let people know as soon as you can that you are a Christian, or else as time goes on you feel less inclined to bring the subject up. I started to go to a mid-week service at lunchtimes, which has really helped me to stay focused on God during the busy week. I would recommend it to anyone. It has also become a talking point with my work colleagues, as they always know where I am off to on Thursday lunchtimes.

Respond

1. What type of colleague will you / do you find most difficult to handle?
2. Think of a frustrating colleague at work. How can you display quick reconciliation rather than growing anger?
3. Think of an attractive colleague at work. How can you display radical decisions rather than casual lust?
4. Think of a nightmare colleague at work. How can you display practical love rather than rightful revenge?

8. AGAINST THE FLOW WITH MONEY

Gerald Ratner, the former head of the high-street jewellers Ratners, became infamous in 1991 when he said that some of the products he sold were cheap because they were 'crap'. The headline in the *Sun* was 'Crapners'. The *Mirror*'s front page shouted out, 'You 22 carat gold mugs!' After this ill-advised comment, Gerald Ratner's whole business took a nosedive and he eventually lost his job.

In his autobiography, it is noticeable how Gerald Ratner's view on money changed after 1991. Talking about life before 1991, Ratner reminisces, 'I remember a friend's mother telling us there was more to life than money and profit. She was right, in a way. But at 21 it was all I was interested in – making money and everything that came with it.'

Compare that with Ratner's current view on money. 'One of the silver linings of losing everything is that you discover the true value of possessions. I'm not saying that money doesn't make you happy, but I do believe that only a certain amount of money makes you happy. Above a certain level you get into the law of diminishing returns. Buying more stuff doesn't make anyone happy in the long term.'[1]

It's a striking change in his view.

But what about our view of money? It's crucial that we think through how to view money and how to use it. Particularly if you are starting out at work, it may be that you have had several years of struggling with student debt, and this is the first time you actually have financial resources available to you. So we need to determine our understanding of money biblically, thoroughly and without delay. The most common view on money in our workplaces today is 'Earn all you can, so you can spend all you can and so you can save all you can – so that when you stop earning, you can still keep spending.'[2] It's the common view of money in our culture, but Jesus' view is very counter-cultural, and so we need to grasp hold of it early on if we're going to work like a trout in the area of money.

Money is a poor investment

> Do not store up for yourselves treasures on earth, where moth and rust destroy, and where thieves break in and steal. But store up for yourselves treasures in heaven, where moth and rust do not destroy, and where thieves do not break in and steal.
> (Matthew 6:19–20)

In our money-obsessed, possession-crazy culture, we so easily put all our focus on the next purchase, but we need to recognize a simple truth: money and possessions don't last for ever.

My first ever car was a beautiful milky-coffee-coloured Renault 5. In fact, it was such a classy car that thieves broke in and stole it. My second ever car, a Renault 5 again (you can see I was going up in the world), was eventually destroyed by rust and, judging by the state of its interior, probably a few moths as well. My cars didn't last for ever.

A colleague of mine recently spoke of the time when his grandmother died. She was confined to her bed in a nursing home for the last months of her life. A few days before she died, he visited her, and looked in her wallet to discover £400 in it. He asked her why she needed all that money with her. 'It makes me feel secure,' was her reply.

There was an American oil millionaire who died and two friends were overheard at his graveside. One said to the other,

'So how much did he actually leave?' The other replied, 'Oh, he left everything.'[3]

We can't take any of our money and possessions with us when we die. Money and possessions are a poor investment because they don't last for ever.

Jesus says that heaven is a good investment. It's the place where we get the best interest rate and where the market will never crash. The most obvious way that we can store up treasures in heaven is by investing in people – because people will be in heaven, while our possessions won't. As Christians, therefore, we should invest in people: the development of our own Christ-like character, helping to meet other people's physical and emotional needs, and encouraging other people to put their trust in Christ for themselves so that they too can be a part of heaven.

The more we believe in the reality of eternity, the less we will feel that we have to hang on to money and possessions in the here and now, and the more we will be prepared to invest in people.

Money is a poor master

If you won £25,000, what would you do with it? Have a think. It's not £25 for Christmas from Aunt Doris; but then again, it's not £25 million, which would completely transform your life and allow you to quit your job right now if you wanted to. Around eight years ago, that was a question I was asked as part of a marriage preparation questionnaire that Susannah and I did to help us think about whether we should get married or not. The idea was to see whether we were compatible, and our answers to the question were revealing.

If you won £25,000, what would you do with it?

Susannah wrote, 'Give it all away.'

I wrote, 'Put it all towards buying a house.'

It's revealing because Jesus says that 'where your treasure is, there your heart will be also' (Matthew 6:21). Where we invest our money reveals to what, or to whom, we're actually committed. The Sermon on the Mount was spoken to people who called themselves Jesus' disciples, and yet again Jesus is alerting us to the possibility that we think we're connected to him when actually we're not.

> No-one can serve two masters. Either he will hate the one and love the other, or he will be devoted to the one and despise the other. You cannot serve both God and Money.
> (Matthew 6:24)

My wife Susannah has a British passport and an Australian passport, and much as she likes to claim that she has allegiance to both countries, you just have to see her supporting the Aussies when we play them at rugby to see that Australia is her master. Even when we beat the Aussies, as we invariably do when it really matters, her master is still Australia. She can't serve both England and Australia.

It's the same with God and money. We cannot serve both. It is impossible. We are either a slave to God or a slave to our money and possessions. It was Martin Luther who wrote that 'there are three conversions necessary: the conversion of the heart, mind and the purse'.

So, as we start out in the workplace and our salaries grow, we need to hear this loud and clear. Are you serving God? Or are you serving money? When the choice is laid before us starkly, we see what fools we are to have any other Master than the one true God. Money doesn't fulfil – Gerald Ratner tells us that. Money certainly doesn't forgive. Whereas in Jesus, God is the only Master who provides both fulfilment and forgiveness.

Poor investment, poor master: is money good for anything?

There was an article in the *Financial Times* recently in which the journalist referred to an interview he conducted with Peter Sutherland, the chairman of BP and Goldman Sachs. This is how the article finished:

> As we looked out from the top floor of the bank's Fleet Street offices, we could enjoy the view of St Paul's and the City of London. 'Ah – God and Mammon!' I observed, predictably. 'Indeed,' replied Mr Sutherland, without missing a beat. 'We need more of both.'[4]

Now we can't have both God and money / Mammon as masters, but Peter Sutherland is totally right. I long for more people to know God, but there's nothing wrong with more money too. Jesus doesn't think it is wrong to make money. Jesus doesn't even think it is wrong to make a lot of money. We're told that Joseph of Arimathea was a rich man. We're told that Jesus was supported financially by a number of wealthy women. It's not even wrong to enjoy the good things of life. Jesus enjoyed plenty of parties in his time. Paul told Timothy that God richly provides us with everything for our enjoyment (1 Timothy 6:17).

Just imagine, if you had a lot of money, you could have your very own servant. You could get them to do all sorts of useful things. Clean your house. Cook your meals. Run errands. Do the ironing. De-moth the car. Or you could just tell them to put their feet up all day and watch TV. You could put your servant to good use or bad use. It's exactly the same with money. Money may be a poor investment and a poor master, but it can be a good servant if we put it to good use.

Broadly speaking, there are three ways in which our money can be used:

1. Spending on us and our dependants (including saving for the future).
2. Giving to gospel work, others and the poor.
3. Paying our taxes.

Obviously it is right to pay all the taxes that we are supposed to pay (Romans 13:6–7; Matthew 22:21). This means that the crucial question about how we use our money is how we divide it up between spending on us and giving it away to others.

Our standard of living

At the start of our working life, we may have debts that need paying off, and it may be a financial struggle. We may have periods later in life when we are also in financial difficulty. In these situations, it is wise to get out of debt as quickly as possible. It's not wrong to borrow money to buy a house, but we do need to make sure that the amounts we have to pay on the mortgage are well within our monthly income. I've seen many people trap themselves in jobs that they struggle in because they have a huge mortgage to pay off. We also need to be very cautious before borrowing money to buy non-essentials and luxuries.

When we don't have debts, we will begin to be able to save some money as our salary comes in, and it's a good thing to save for the future. In fact, the New Testament tells us that anyone who doesn't provide for his immediate family is worse than an unbeliever (1 Timothy 5:8), and that we should not be a burden on anyone (2 Thessalonians 3:7–13). So it's a good thing to pay money into a pension now, even if your retirement is over forty years away. I haven't done the maths, but I'm told that someone who saves £100 a month in their twenties alone will have a larger pension on their retirement than someone who saves £100 a month between the ages of thirty and sixty-five.[5]

As we think through debts, saving and spending, it's important that we recognize where to draw the line between a necessity and a luxury. As we look around at the culture in which we live and work, we can very quickly develop a mentality that says it's a necessity to own a house, or to have a holiday abroad, or to own an iPod, or to be able to buy clothes with designer labels, or to go out to nice restaurants, or to buy coffees from Starbucks. But in the Bible, the line drawn between necessity and luxury comes at a completely different level. Writing to Timothy, Paul says that we should be content with the necessities of food and clothing – that's where he draws the line (1 Timothy 6:8). It's startlingly basic. By that definition, owning a house is a luxury and having a choice of high-quality food or clothes is also a luxury.

Now, I'm not saying it's wrong to own a house or to buy food from Marks and Spencer – but we also need to realize that there is no reason why our standard of living should change over time. As our income grows, our huge temptation is to enlarge what we think of as a necessity. We so easily increase our standard of living as our income goes up, when actually, once we're meeting our needs and the needs of our immediate family, there is no reason to increase our standard of living at all.

For our money to be put to good use, we need to be clear on our right standard of living.

Our focus for living

A recent advertising campaign for Ikea, the king of flat-pack furniture, asks us, 'Do you live in a house or a home?' It's a good question. What should matter most for us is not what we do to our house – the new kitchen units from Ikea; the new sofa from Ikea; the new home office from Ikea . . . Those things shouldn't be our main focus. It's not about what we do to our house, but about what we do in our home – the marriages and families we build; the hospitality we show; the friendships we foster; the conversations we have. We live in homes, not houses.

Or take our work. What should matter most for us about our jobs is not the salary we get, the private health plan we're entitled to, the promotion we're offered – but what we do in our work; the integrity we show; the conversations about Christ we have; the work well done; the compassion we show to that struggling colleague.

When we have that mentality, then we are able to let money be a good servant to us. It won't mean that we will all be poor, but it will mean that when we use money to buy things, we do it with the right goal in mind. So I think of someone I know who owns a big house. It's huge, but he is hugely generous with it. On the Christian holidays for teenagers I used to help at, the leaders' planning weekends would always be at his house, and he would have fifty people descending to meet and eat and sleep. His focus was not on having a big house as a status symbol. His focus was on having a big house as a means of being generous to others. He had taken on board Paul's words to the rich:

> Command those who are rich in this present world not to be arrogant nor to put their hope in wealth, which is so uncertain, but to put their hope in God, who richly provides us with everything for our enjoyment. Command them to do good, to be rich in good deeds, and to be generous and willing to share.
> (1 Timothy 6:17–18)

When our focus is like that, we will be people who are giving as well as looking to our own needs. Giving of our possessions. Giving of our time. Giving of our skills. And giving of our money.

If we are going to be generous in the giving of our money, our giving needs to be planned and prioritized. We won't just drift into it. This is what Ken Costa, the chairman of Alpha International and a leading investment banker, writes about his giving:

> Once my wife and I have decided on the total amount it is right to give, we slice the cake in a fairly disciplined manner. The lion's share goes to our church. We trust the leadership to use the money wisely and feel responsible as congregation members both to help pay for boring running costs (such as heating, lighting and administration) and to contribute to the church's vision. The next slice goes to other local or global Christian organizations that attract us personally. We are particularly keen to support evangelism before general charitable giving, as these wider initiatives have a much bigger potential pool of donors. In one sense we treat our giving like any other investment and make a point of listening to our 'investment reports' (also known as missionary feedback). We find it very encouraging when we recognize in the lives changed, the yield on our money and our prayers.[6]

For our money to be put to good use, we need to be clear on the right focus for living.

What is your focus?

Most Christians correctly know that money itself is not the root of all evil, but it is the *love* of money that is the root of all evil (1 Timothy 6:10). If I asked, 'Do you love money?' you'd know what you should say. But what about a different question: 'Do you want to get rich?' Can you answer that – honestly?

If, like me, you often want to get rich, then take on the challenge of what the Bible says to you and me.

> People who want to get rich fall into temptation and a trap and into many foolish and harmful desires that plunge men into ruin and destruction. For the love of money is a root of all kinds of evil. Some people, eager for money, have wandered from the faith and pierced themselves with many griefs.
> (1 Timothy 6:9–10)

In the Bible there are around 500 verses about prayer, but there are more than 2,350 verses on how we use money, and yet we very rarely talk about money or encourage each other to examine our hearts and our finances. I recently read an article in which the writer said, 'After 15 years as a pastor, I've found it much easier to talk to men about their sex lives than about their finances.'[7]

And so, like trout, we need to go against the flow. We need to talk about money rather than ignoring it. We need to talk about it in our churches, our small groups, our families, our accountability groups, with Christian friends and Christian colleagues. And then we need to develop the focus that Jesus wants us to have.

In AD 1000, 186 years after the death of Emperor Charlemagne, officials reopened the great king's tomb and encountered an amazing sight. In the midst of all the finery buried with him – the gold, the jewels, the priceless treasure – was the skeleton of King Charlemagne, still seated upon his throne and with the crown still on his head. On his lap there lay an open Bible and one bony finger rested on these words: 'What good is it for a man to gain the whole world, yet forfeit his soul?' (Mark 8:36)[8]

For Emperor Charlemagne, it wasn't actually relevant how much gold and treasure was accumulated around him. He couldn't keep that beyond the grave. Nor can we. Our focus shouldn't be on storing up treasures on earth for ourselves, but on focusing on things that will last into eternity.

On its own, money should be seen neither as something negative which might contaminate us, nor as something positive which will be a blessing to all. It all depends on our attitude to how we use our money.

Money can be a good servant as long as we are guided in how we put it to use by the Good Master – the Lord Jesus Christ.

Recap

8. Against the flow with money

Money is a poor investment
Money is a poor master

So ... is money good for anything?

With a right **standard of living** ...

... and with a **right focus for living** ...

Money is a good servant

Relate

Name: Tony Chin
Job: Investment analyst

In my job I earn a decent amount of money – some would say more than decent! On top of that, I work with money day in and day out. My role is to analyse industries, and companies within them – at present, oil, gas and automotive industries – with a view to picking the stocks for inclusion in portfolios we manage on behalf of clients, in a way that gives our clients superior risk-adjusted returns.

I believe the subject of money is a challenging one for all Christians, and especially so for those working in financial services. I am no exception. I know well Jesus' command that we cannot serve two masters, but still I find it tough to make sure that, day in, day out, it is God I'm serving, not money.

In the last year or so as the markets fell back, I found myself worrying increasingly about my family's finances, including how much we were spending and how we were going to sustain the lifestyle to which we had become accustomed. I also recognized that my obligations to support family living outside the UK, where currencies were appreciating sharply, were rising by the day. I was getting drawn to the next piece of financial news in the media in an effort to do a better job and get paid more to compensate for what was going on in the markets. Seeking the Lord's wisdom became a secondary priority, and so it has been an ongoing desire for me recently to ensure that I actually do what God's word tells me – not just read it or listen to it and then forget about it.

I have been abundantly blessed in so many ways – with my family and my friends, but also in terms of the remuneration that comes from my job. One key way I ensure that I am serving God, not money, is by taking seriously Paul's command to the rich – 'to do good, to be rich in good deeds, and to be generous and willing to share' (1 Timothy 6:18). My wife and I try to share our gifts with others, and in particular with those who are involved in serving in our church, and with those we want to come to know Christ for themselves. My wife loves cooking and we enjoy good wines. We enjoy the company and fellowship of our friends and we try to reach out by hosting dinner parties where we hope good conversation and discussion about topical issues will take place.

What I am not good at is contributing increasingly to the state's coffers with the same willing spirit I have in supporting the work of the church or sharing our gifts with others. This translates into a daily struggle because I know that the Bible tells us to love others as ourselves, but also to pay our taxes.

Above all, my ongoing desire is, whilst thanking God for what he has given me and enjoying it, to make sure that I don't place my hope in wealth, which is so uncertain, but rather place my hope in God (1 Timothy 6:17).

Respond

1. If you won £25,000, what would you do with it?
2. Do you need to change your standard of living or your focus for living?
3. How can you 'do good . . . be rich in good deeds, and . . . be generous and willing to share'? Give some practical examples.

9. AGAINST THE FLOW WITH STRESS

One of my closest friends, Andy, is passionate about free-diving. This sport, if you can call it such a thing, involves seeing how deep you can dive just by holding your breath and diving down. The other weekend Andy went off to Dorset to spend all day Saturday and all day Sunday in a giant cylinder full of water – a cylinder about 5 metres in diameter and 30 metres deep, so a bit like an ant in a tube of Smarties.

Now free-diving has two main challenges. The first is being able to hold your breath for a long time. Andy can hold his breath for four or five minutes. I tried to see how long I could do it for, and conked out after about fifteen seconds. The second, more critical challenge is being able to manage the greater pressure that is exerted on you as you go further and further down into the water. Andy has had to learn how to equalize the pressure in his ears, sinuses and mask so that he is able to keep going down further into the water despite the pressure increasing.

Andy's a very capable swimmer – he was captain of the Cambridge University water polo team – but I've got to say I think he is an absolute nutter doing free-diving. Yet free-diving is actually a very helpful picture of what many of us experience in our day-to-day working lives.

There are times in life when we find ourselves experiencing increased pressure. Not from diving deep down into a giant cylinder of water while looking like a mermaid, but just from the circumstances of life at any given time. We may experience increased pressure in a relationship, or because we're moving house, or because we're ill or we have financial worries, or just because we're late to catch a train. Or indeed, we may feel increased pressure because of what is going on for us at work. All of those are examples of when we're like that free-diver, diving deep into the water and experiencing increased pressure.

Stress can be defined as 'the reaction of mind and body to increased pressure'. It can be a positive thing, but as a negative concept, stress happens when we feel we are unable to cope with the increased pressure we face. That can happen in many different ways at work:

- When we start the job and feel out of our depth.
- When there is too much work landed on us with unrealistic deadlines.
- When we have a nightmare relationship with the boss and just don't know how to cope.
- When we feel undervalued in our job, and we don't know what to do.
- When we feel the threat of unemployment and we can't see any other options.

Those can be times when we feel unable to cope with the increased pressure, and it leads to us having a negative reaction of mind and body.

When we are stressed, the stress can show itself in the mind – psychologically. We become distracted. We are unable to concentrate. We get anxious. We become aggressive. We become irrational. We become self-absorbed. We lose perspective. Stress can also show itself in the body – physically. We can't eat. We can't sleep. We feel a tightness around the chest. When I'm too stressed, I start feeling tight around my left shoulder. It's not a heart attack, but it's a warning sign to me that I'm starting not to cope. Stress can affect anyone and everyone. Stress afflicts even the finest and most able.

The effects of stress are no small thing.

- Research from Harvard University says that work stress is as harmful to health as smoking or taking no exercise.[1]
- The Institute of Personnel and Development says that in the UK, 6.5 million working days are lost to sickness due to stress.[2]
- BUPA reckon that 270,000 people take time off work every day due to stress.[3]
- Stress has overtaken the common cold as the biggest cause of sick leave from work.[4]

In fact, pretty much all of us will have struggled with stress at some point or other, and there will be many reading this book for whom the challenge of stress is a live issue right now.

Tom is a talented guy. He is very bright and training to be an accountant. When I met up with him recently, he told me he had been in tears at least once a week, every week in the previous month, because he just couldn't cope with the stress of his work. In terms of the definition for stress, the increased pressure in his work was having a negative effect on his mind and his body. It was regularly causing him to be sobbing in the loo at his workplace.

So what's the solution when we feel stressed because of an increased pressure? Can the pressure be managed as Andy manages and equalizes the increased pressure as he dives down? Stress management, as it's called, is big business. If you look into it, you will read of various techniques for managing stress such as meditation, progressive relaxation, cognitive therapy, stress balls, time management. You'll read of little tips such as accepting offers of practical help, talking to someone, taking a holiday, and hitting a pillow to let off steam. My favourite tip for stress that I've read about involves spraying lemon extract into the air because, according to research, computer keyboard errors have been shown to fall by over 50% when lemon is diffused into the office atmosphere.[5]

Now, I don't want to knock all these things I've just mentioned – although there's no free sample of lemon extract available with this book. But I do think there's a big flaw with most contemporary stress management. Most remedies try to deal with the symptoms of stress that we can see on the surface, whereas Jesus' teaching goes straight to the underlying cause. He tells us how we can manage our stress at the deep, underlying, causal level.

As Jesus preached the Sermon on the Mount, he drew a division between two groups of people. Not a division between those who face stressful situations and those who don't, because we all face stressful situations. But a division based on how we cope with those stressful situations. The challenge is that Jesus says, when it comes to the area of worry and stress, many of us who think of ourselves as very religious and Christian actually act just like those who are not Christians.

But, as well as challenging us, Jesus also offers us huge help in the Sermon on the Mount, because he gives us stress management in three dimensions.

The intellectual dimension

In the first dimension of Jesus' stress management, he simply wants to give us a lesson in logic. He wants us to use our brains and see that worry is a waste of time. 'Who of you by worrying can add a single hour to his life?' says Jesus (Matthew 6:27). We can't add anything to our lives by worrying. Worry can only subtract from our lives by causing things like ill health. But that's not all. Jesus continues by telling us, 'Do not worry about tomorrow, for tomorrow will worry about itself. Each day has enough trouble of its own' (Matthew 6:34). He reminds us that worry is about tomorrow, but it is experienced today. When we worry, we are stressed in the present about some event that may, or may not, happen in the future. Writing about this verse, John Stott comments, 'If our fear does not materialise, we have worried once for nothing; if it does materialise, we have worried twice instead of once. In both cases it is foolish; worry doubles trouble.'[6] It's just a matter of logic. It's a waste of time and effort to worry.

The emotional dimension

> Look at the birds of the air; they do not sow or reap or store away in barns, and yet your heavenly Father feeds them. Are you not much more valuable than they?
> (Matthew 6:26)

When Jesus tells us not to worry, it is not to be seen as an excuse for idleness or carelessness. Birds aren't idle. They work very hard to get their food. They give thought to the future too by storing food and building nests and migrating in the winter. Birds work hard, but they don't worry.

> Said the robin to the sparrow
> I should really like to know
> Why these anxious human beings
> Rush about and worry so.

> Said the sparrow to the robin:
> Friend I think that it must be
> That they have no heavenly Father.
> Such as cares for you and me.[7]

The birds trust their Creator in a way that we human beings seem incapable of doing.

When my daughter Daisy was a few months shy of her second birthday, we went on a family holiday in Cornwall with my parents. She loved going in the sea so much that her grandparents bought Daisy her very own tiny surfboard. She was a little confused about it – she referred to it as her ironing board. But despite the confusion in vocabulary, she loved going surfing. I'd hold her on the board and she'd catch some small waves in the water. In fact, she loved it so much that again and again, when we weren't in the sea, Daisy just ran into the water, pointed out to sea and shouted, 'Out, out!' – and headed straight out.

Obviously this was not entirely safe, so I'd have to charge into the water after her, and then out to sea we would go together, with me holding Daisy's hand as she walked out right up to her neck, with me pulling her up out of the water as each wave reached her so that she wouldn't go completely under.

This kamikaze behaviour is partly because Daisy seems to be a natural adrenaline junkie thrill-seeker (I don't know where she gets it from). But partly it's because she trusts me, her dad.

Daisy didn't mind charging into the sea when she was only twenty months old and couldn't swim.

Daisy didn't mind walking almost out of her depth in the sea.

Daisy didn't mind waves much bigger than her coming her way.

She trusted that I would look after her. She trusted me because, imperfect though I am, she knows she has a dad who loves her and values her.

How much more should we as Christians trust our perfect Heavenly Father?

I won't always be able to protect Daisy in everything she gets up to in life. I won't be around all the time. I'll make mistakes and do or say the wrong thing. But we, as Christians, have a great God – a Heavenly Father who looks after us perfectly. Someone who won't necessarily wrap us in cotton wool, but who will always be with us and will always do what is best for us and care for us in the best way. Someone who is more than big enough to take care of every little detail of our lives about which we get so worried and stressed. If we start actually believing that, then we will be able to manage our stress far better, because we will not be people of little faith in a little God.

Not only do we need to hold on to how great our God is, but we also need to realize our own great value. When Jesus talks about the birds, he says, 'Are you not much more valuable than they?' When he turns his attention to the lilies of the field, he says, 'If that is how God clothes the grass of the field, which is here today and tomorrow is thrown into the fire, will he not much more clothe you, O you of little faith?' (Matthew 6:30) Above all, Jesus wants us to realize how much more valuable and precious we are to God than anything else in his creation.

Jesus tells us to look at the birds, the flowers, the grass of the field, and we all love to look at the beautiful things in this world. But so often we go and draw the wrong conclusion. We think that God must really care about that beautiful view. Then we look at ourselves in the mirror and in most cases it's not such a beautiful view, and so we end up not being able to believe that God cares for us and all the details of our little lives.

What fools we are for having such little faith! It cost God just a word to create this world, but it cost God the life of Jesus to bring you and me into relationship with him. Christ's first priority in his death was not to rescue the Asian tiger or the

Grand Canyon. Christ's first priority in his death was to rescue you and me. That's how much more valuable we are to God.

When we combine the greatness of God with the great value he places on us, it's then that we feel the full force of the emotional dimension of Jesus' stress management. We start to realize that Jesus wants us to savour how valuable we are to our Heavenly Father. He wants us to let our emotions be actively buoyed up by God's greatness and by our great value.

That's certainly what I need to do. I get stressed and I worry far too much – about the future; about provision for the family and myself; about decisions to be made. I worry. I need to grasp this second dimension of Jesus' stress management more than most.

The practical dimension

> So do not worry, saying, 'What shall we eat?' or 'What shall
> we drink?' or 'What shall we wear?' For the pagans run after
> all these things, and your heavenly Father knows that you
> need them. But seek first his kingdom and his righteousness,
> and all these things will be given to you as well.
> (Matthew 6:31–33)

Recently I was walking to a meeting with someone in London when, as I was standing on a corner, some police motorbikes pulled up directly in front of me, stopped all the traffic, and allowed three smart black cars to drive past without having to stop. As the cars turned the corner right next to me, who should I see through the darkened windows of the back seat of the first car but the British prime minister, Gordon Brown. He had some papers on his lap and was talking to someone on his mobile phone.

Now, I don't know what you would think in such a situation, but, high-brow thinker that I am, my first thought as Gordon and his entourage sped away was, 'Lucky Gordon – he doesn't need to worry about traffic jams when driving through London.'

It's true. With the police stopping all the traffic, the prime minister doesn't need to worry about getting held up or being late for a meeting. Rather, it enables him to worry about more important matters, whatever his papers and his phone conversation were all about – the fight against terrorism, or the credit crunch perhaps?

Jesus' third dimension of stress management is telling us a similar thing. The prime minister doesn't worry about the traffic, and this enables him to worry about the more important thing on his agenda. Jesus says to us that we are not to worry about what we will eat, drink or wear, so that we can worry instead about the more important thing – his kingdom and his righteousness.

In one way, we have been made to worry and feel stress. We're not supposed just to float aimlessly through life. The problem is that so often our focus is on the wrong things. Jesus says that the practical dimension to stress management is to switch our perspective. Our salary, our health, our prospects, our children's prospects are so often what dominate our thinking. Jesus tells us to switch our focus to the things that matter most: 'Seek first his kingdom and his righteousness.'

Now, don't get me wrong. Jesus is not saying we shouldn't be concerned about anything else at all in life. Jesus thinks it is right for us to have a priority of concerns. He thinks that life is more important than food and that the body is more important than clothes (Matthew 6:25). So it is right to be concerned about other things and to have a priority of concern. So often, however, we have the wrong thing as top priority.

Whether it is our promotion or our fear of being made redundant, whether it is our relationship with our boss or our relationship with our boyfriend/girlfriend – so often something else is dominating our thinking, when the number one spot, the thing of first importance, should be seeking first God's kingdom and his righteousness.

Seeking God's kingdom is all about desiring the spread of Jesus, who is the King of the kingdom. It means wanting Jesus to rule as King in all areas of our own lives, and wanting him to be King in other people's lives too. Seeking God's righteousness is linked to this, but perhaps has more of a focus on encouraging God's standards in society. It's not so much about the rule of God as about our right living for God.

So Jesus says it is those two things – God's kingdom and God's righteousness – which matter most. He actually says that if we do put God's kingdom and God's righteousness first, then the rest of life begins to fall into place. All these other things do have a place in our life, just not first place.

Which way are you flowing?

As you go through your working life, it is likely that there will be times of stress. Even if you have not entered the workplace yet, it is likely that you have experienced stressful times in life already. There may even be times of stress when we need to get specialist help from a doctor or a counsellor. But in those times when we feel like that free-diver experiencing increased pressure, we will survive far better if we have been continually looking to apply Jesus' three dimensions of stress management.

For some people in some highly stressful work situations, the increased pressure may be so huge that the only thing to do is to get right away from the pressure, swim back to the surface, and quit that job. But for the majority of us, even in the times of increased pressure in our work, it will mean remaining in our working situation. Remaining, but in our thinking – 'seeing' that worry is a waste of time. Remaining, but in our feelings – savouring how valuable we are to our Heavenly Father. Remaining, but in our actions – switching to focusing on the things that matter most.

Jesus' three dimensions are the best stress management technique on the market today. Yet no amount of money can buy this stress management package. It's simply a free bonus gift for the person who trusts in the one true God.

It may be the best stress management technique, but just as with our character, our relationships and our money, this is going very much against the flow of the workplace. It's hugely counter-cultural – and so it's a massive challenge to keep living it out. That's why we need to remember that as we work like a trout, we may often be swimming against the flow of the workplace, but we will always be swimming with the flow and in the currents of our Heavenly Father who created us.

Recap

9. Against the flow with stress

1. The intellectual dimension
See that worry is a waste of time

2. The emotional dimension
Savour God's greatness and your great value to him

3. The practical dimension
Switch to focusing on the things that matter most

 Which way are you flowing?

Relate

Name: Kiren Rajakumar
Occupation: Personal assistant

It was the worst experience I have ever had at work. Initially I was very keen, excited and wanted to learn. No matter how strange or unreasonable a situation was, I kept thinking, 'Just keep trying.' I hadn't realized how fragile the human psyche is. The experience had touched parts of me that I thought were immovable and untouchable. It eroded my inner strength, dignity and confidence. For someone who had survived some knocks already, it left me startled at the person I was becoming. I had stuck it out for over four years and have often wondered if I should have left my job as a business analyst sooner.

It was always easier to see the issues in the people or situations around me, yet I came to realize that I had many lessons to learn. I would certainly have preferred to have learned them in a less painful manner, yet I think many of the lessons will only have been learned in that situation. Thankfully, while that part of my life was spiralling downwards, I was also rediscovering my faith, a real relationship with God and an understanding that his grace is sufficient (2 Corinthians 12:9). It was a done deal – Jesus had taken care of it.

I have come out of it realizing that if that was what it was like for God to have taken me through that lesson . . . ever so gently because in each situation I could still think of a far harsher alternative (though it really did seem about as bad as it could get) . . . then I would much rather walk with him through every situation than not to have known him. I would rather go through this, have known him and been able to draw closer to him than not.

Towards the end of this time of immense stress at work, I received one very valuable piece of advice: to deal with the increasing pressure and stress at work, I needed to put myself in situations or involve myself in activities which would counter that stress or pressure so as to keep me on an even keel.

I left the job as a business analyst about a year ago, not having another job to go to. Having taken quite a knock, I looked for and took on temporary work. Every job I have had since then seems to have addressed a particular bit of me that needed mending. Six months later I was in a permanent role as a personal assistant. So this is the ongoing rebuilding, or re-engineering, of Kiren Rajakumar and it's amazing to see God at work in me.

Respond

1. What particular things cause you stress? How well do you think you handle stress?
2. Which of the three dimensions of Jesus' stress management do you most need to remind yourself about in times of stress?
3. What situations at work cause you to face 'increased pressure'? How can you deal with them? Are there ways in which you can act to minimize the pressure increase?

PART 4

WORK LIKE A TRUMPET

Flourishing for God in the workplace

So far, with the treadmill, the trampoline and the trout, we've looked at what the workplace is like (Part 1), what some of its challenges and pitfalls are for the Christian (Part 2), and how we as Christians might best operate at work so that our faith survives (Part 3). The aim is that these three parts will encourage you in why and how you can work without wilting in your faith as you go through your entire working life.

However, if I finished the book here, there would be a problem. A big problem. God doesn't want us spending over forty years of our lives just keeping our head above water as far as our faith is concerned. Of course he doesn't want us wilting altogether in the trials of working life, but his goal for us is more than mere faith survival.

While work is a negative challenge to negotiate, it is also a positive opportunity to grasp. Too often when Christians think about work, we can talk very negatively and defensively. We focus on the struggles, the difficulties, the temptations and the woes. That is right in part, but if it is all we say, we'll discover that we have a very lop-sided view which will be detrimental both to ourselves and to others. The truth is that there is pleasure and joy to be had, both in doing our work and in the relationships we form while we are at work. There is delight at being a part of God's gift of work. We can be joyful about it, because in amongst the challenges and struggles, there are significant, exciting opportunities.

Earlier this year I was asked to join a discussion which would be recorded and sent to the leadership teams of all churches in the New Wine network in the UK. The subject of our discussion was 'God at Work', and the three people in the discussion were me, Mark Greene from the London Institute for Contemporary Christianity, and Paul Pease, the pastor of Hook Evangelical Church. I'd never met Paul before, but I was really struck by the mission statement that he had coined for the church where he served. It was this: 'We aim to be a place where people are built up in Christ to survive and thrive on the front line, and the front line is wherever we spend most of the time.'

That mission statement is a good commentary for this book. We've looked so far at how to survive at work, but now we are turning our attention towards how to thrive at work. Part 4 is all about seizing the opportunities so that we are people who not only don't wilt, but also flourish in our faith while being in the workplace.

That's where the trumpet fits in.

In my thinking about this subject, the trumpet seems a good picture to hold on to as we seek a renewed vision for our work which encompasses the thriving as well as the surviving, the flourishing as well as the not-wilting.

Personally, I've always had a mixed relationship with trumpets. As a small child, I thought the trumpet was the classiest instrument to play. Eventually, aged nine, I persuaded my parents to let me have trumpet lessons. After only three weeks of lessons, my music teacher rather charmingly told me that the trumpet and I should part company. I can remember his words to this day: 'Jago, your mouth is too big for the trumpet.' And that was the end of that.

My relationship with the trumpet lasted three weeks. I hope your relationship with it will last a good deal longer. As you enter the workplace, or as you continue in it, the trumpet is a means of helping us flourish in our faith while we are at work.

10. GLORIFYING GOD AT WORK

What has a trumpet got to do with work?

Work is a trumpet fanfare

A trumpet fanfare is used to declare the existence of someone important. When the Queen walks into a room there is often a trumpet fanfare and everyone will stand up to acknowledge her. Our work is like that. As we work, we are declaring the existence of someone important. Our work is a trumpet fanfare to God. In Paul's first letter to the Corinthians, he writes, 'So whether you eat or drink or whatever you do, do it all for the glory of God' (1 Corinthians 10:31). That has to include our work. Whatever we do, whether we are an accountant or an air stewardess, whether we are a builder or a barrister, we are to do it all for the glory of God. Our work is to be a fanfare to him.

It really is *whatever* we do. It's not as if God approves of some jobs more than others. In chapters 8 – 10 of 1 Corinthians, Paul's whole focus has been on the amazing freedom the Corinthians had in relation to eating food sacrificed to idols. He speaks of how the Corinthians were not closer to or further away from God depending on whether they did or did not eat the food (1 Corinthians 8:8). But he could just as easily have been speaking about what work we do. We are no worse or no better depending on the type of job we do. What job we have doesn't bring us nearer to or further away from God.

In Christian circles there can often seem to be an underlying hierarchy of jobs. As Mark Greene comments, 'All Christians are born equal, but 'full-time' Christians are more equal than others.'[1] I can remember that some Christians were very concerned that I was 'selling out' by going into the world of management consultancy when I left university. Their thought process was along these lines: 'If you're not going to be a church worker, which is the best thing to be, then you should really be a doctor or teacher or social worker. They do good. Management consultants don't.'

That's not what it says in 1 Corinthians. Whatever we do, we are to do it to the glory of God. And there are plenty of times when church workers do not bring glory to God in what they do, and equally there are plenty of times when management consultants do bring glory to God in what they do.

That has got to spur us on to flourish in our faith at work. What we do – whatever job we are in – is a means of bringing glory to God. What a privilege! Our work is a trumpet fanfare.

There is a challenge as well, though. Tootling out a jolly little trumpet fanfare to God through our work sounds quite fun, doesn't it? Yet, if we work well in our jobs – even if we work morally, honourably and efficiently, even if we work with integrity, with creativity and with courtesy – if we do all that but that's all we do, we'll actually be playing a fanfare that will bring glory to ourselves, not to God.

It's obvious, really. If you do really well at work, your boss is unlikely to declare, 'Praise be to God!' In fact, you'd probably be flat out on the floor with surprise if they did. Your boss is much more likely to say, 'Praise be to Mary / Toby (or whatever your name is)!' You are the one who will get the glory. So, for God's glory to be more fully recognized in our workplaces, our work needs to include a verbal witness about God. Otherwise our work will end up being more to the glory of ourselves than to the glory of God.

Work is a trumpet melody

> So whether you eat or drink or whatever you do, do it all for
> the glory of God. Do not cause anyone to stumble, whether
> Jews, Greeks or the church of God – even as I try to please
> everybody in every way. For I am not seeking my own good
> but the good of many, so that they may be saved. Follow my
> example, as I follow the example of Christ.
> (1 Corinthians 10:31 – 11:1)

If the overall trumpet fanfare is to work for the glory of God,
what is the actual melody that is being played out? As Paul
writes to the Corinthians, the melody seems to revolve around
the theme of us using the amazing freedom we have as
Christians to actually *restrict* our freedom out of love for
others. Just as the trumpet has three valves to produce all the
notes that make up the melody, so Paul outlines three means
of us playing out this melody in our workplaces.

Valve One is that we are to work so non-Christians (Jews
and Greeks in Paul's passage) don't stumble. We need to be
clear on whether there is anything that we do at work which
blocks people from coming to Jesus.

In my old job, there was a time when my department went
on a two-day team-building session in the Cotswolds. There
were about fifteen of us there, and at one point in the
programme we had about an hour when we had to spend
five minutes with each person on the team in turn, and we
had to tell the other person very briefly how we saw them.
We had to list their strengths and their weaknesses.

I'll never forget what one person said to me. As is always
the way, he said the nice things first. But once he had buttered
me up, he dropped the bombshell. 'Jago – you're too focused
on whatever you're doing. Often I'll come and ask you a

question, and you give me the answer, but you're not interested in me and don't chat to me and just see how I'm doing. Jago – you're too focused.'

I was really shaken and ashamed by what he said to me. At the time I was the only Christian in this small department and, as far as I knew, the only Christian this guy knew – and his impression of Christians and Christ from me was that he was of little importance. He felt that I didn't have time for him. My actions were causing a stumbling block to this person coming to Christ.

I would urge you to do a bit of regular assessment on the melody you are playing with valve one of the trumpet. If your colleagues look at you and, because you behave in a certain way, they don't want to have anything to do with Christianity, then you need to ask God to help you change, just as I needed to. Maybe it's your foul temper. Maybe it's not being a team player – you just bunk off work early even when everyone else is still slaving away. Maybe, as it was for me, you are so focused on getting the job done that you lack any concern for the well-being of your colleagues.

Valve Two is that we need to work so that Christians (the church of God) don't stumble. In order to play a melody bringing glory to God in our work, we need to make sure that we're not doing anything which causes other Christians to stumble in their faith.

Take Sam. He decided not to drink alcohol with his colleagues after work. He was fine with having a glass or two, and then stopping. But a Christian colleague of his often came out in the group and ended up having far too much to drink and getting plastered. Because this Christian colleague really struggled with alcohol, Sam thought it better that he didn't drink any alcohol at all so that he wouldn't in any way be a cause of his colleague stumbling by getting drunk.

Finally, *Valve Three*, which will help us to complete our trumpet melody at work, is that we work so that everybody is pleased – 'even as I try to please everybody in every way' (1 Corinthians 10:33). Now in one way this valve is obvious. At work, we don't want to be known to be awkward for the sake of being awkward. There's nothing worse than that for the cause of Christ. Christians should be people who are good to employ.

Yet it might also come as a bit of a surprise. We might be tempted to think that Paul has suddenly lost his backbone and his principles, telling us to be people-pleasers rather than God-pleasers. Paul's next sentence answers this fear. He says that we should not be seeking our own good, but 'the good of many, so that they may be saved'. That is the key. Paul is willing to please everybody in every way, not for his own good, or his own career advancement, or his own reputation at work, but for the good of others. In fact, for their eternal good – 'that they may be saved'.

Earlier in his letter to the Corinthians, Paul has actually outlined this thinking in more depth in a paragraph of the Bible which I think is amazing for its passion and desire for people's eternal destiny:

> Though I am free and belong to no man, I make myself a slave to everyone, to win as many as possible. To the Jews I became like a Jew, to win the Jews. To those under the law I became like one under the law (though I myself am not under the law), so as to win those under the law. To those not having the law I became like one not having the law (though I am not free from God's law but am under Christ's law), so as to win those not having the law. To the weak I became weak, to win the weak. I have become all things to all men so that by all possible means I might save

some. I do all this for the sake of the gospel, that I may share in its blessings.

(1 Corinthians 9:19–23)

Paul is ready to be all things to all people – so that some may be saved.

So will we stay late at work to help a colleague with a task they still have to do? It's not going to be for our own good, but it is going to be for the good of our colleague.

Will we play squash with a colleague once a week, even if it means missing out on playing football with our mates from church, and even if we think squash is such a 'last millennium' sport? Will we do it so that we can spend time with our colleague, so that we might win that person for Christ?

Will we admit to our colleagues our own struggles at work, or our own struggles outside work, even though it makes us look less capable and less ambitious? After all, that's the truth about us, and it will help our colleagues in turn to be real and honest with us.

Will we stay in our job rather than moving to a new, exciting opportunity? Will we do that because in our current job there is someone we know well who seems very close to becoming a Christian, and we want to be able to win them for Christ, even if it means forfeiting this amazing new job possibility?

Will we become all things to all people, so that by all possible means we might save some?

Of course it's not always easy. Don't I know how so often at work it's tempting just to look to our own agenda and to look for our own comfort and ease, rather than thinking what is best for others? And things aren't always clear cut. Sometimes what is best for the people who work for us may not be what is best for the people we work for. There will of course be tensions.

Yet, this is the melody that God wants us to play at work, using all three of the trumpet's valves:

- Valve One – Work so that non-Christians don't stumble.
- Valve Two – Work so that Christians don't stumble.
- Valve Three – Work so that everybody is pleased.

Work is a trumpet call

The trumpet is often used as a wake-up call. It's used in the army and in the Bible – to call people to wake up and to alert them to an impending danger. If we are going to thrive positively in our faith while at work, we need to see that one of our roles there is to be a trumpet call. Our lives at work are to be a spiritual wake-up call to those with whom we work, urging them to trust in Jesus for themselves so that they might be saved.

Please don't misunderstand me. I'm not saying that we must talk about why Jesus died on the cross with a colleague once a week or we are of no use in our workplace. That's completely untrue. There will be times when we get to speak about Jesus quite a bit, and there will be times when we don't speak much about him for a long period of time when at work. But too often we can lose our focus on the fact that one reason for us being at work is, by God's grace, to wake people up to realize who Jesus is – so that they might trust in him and be saved from an eternity in hell.

It is very easy to get so wrapped up in our job that we forget there is a work that, as Christians, we are all involved in – over and above editing that programme, or mending that bit of rail track, or defending that client, or caring for that sick person, or driving that bus, or whatever it is that we do. Of course, we are to edit the programme well, we are to mend the rail track effectively, we are to defend the client to the best of our ability, we are to care for the person in hospital with all compassion, we are to drive the bus safely. But at the same time we are to be focused on calling people to Christ. All of us – whatever job we do. Take Fiona, a full-time mum. She told me that when others ask her what she does, although she always answers, 'I'm a full-time mum,' she tries to remind herself each time that 'I'm not just a mum. I'm working to raise a new generation to know and love Jesus.'

If we don't try to call our colleagues to Christ, who will? For most of us, we will be the only Christian our colleagues know well. Our workplaces are often mission fields far more needy than countries visited by missionaries. In the management consultancy firm where I used to work, I reckon there were 40–80 Bible-believing Christians out of 8,000 employees. That's 0.5–1% of the population. Compare that to countries where we might expect missionaries to go: Nepal, 1.9%; Iraq, 1.55%; Saudi Arabia is a whopping 4.5%.[2]

I was in the front line of working for God in my job as a management consultant. But six years ago, when I moved to work as a Workplace Minister of a church, I moved to the back line. In that job I was supporting others like you who were in the front line, blowing their trumpets for God as they called others to him.

A vision for work

I remember one New Year's Eve when I was a student and I was in my car (the bright red Renault 5 that met its end through rust and moths) driving down the M4 motorway. It was raining tigers and Great Danes.

Picture the scene. My windscreen wipers are on the highest speed setting, going like the clappers as I try to see just a few yards in front of the car. Suddenly the wiper on the passenger side just flies off. It's gone. It's a little alarming. But I tell myself it's OK. After all, I don't really need to see out of that side of the windscreen and I can still see straight in front of me.

On I drive in the torrential rain for a few more minutes. Suddenly my one remaining wiper directly in front of me doesn't fly off, but it does wrap itself round my wing mirror.

So there I am, driving down the M4. In the torrential rain. On New Year's Eve. With no windscreen wipers. With the window wound down and my head sticking out as I tried desperately to see where I was going. It wasn't a happy experience.

Being in the car with no windscreen wipers is a little bit like the way many of us feel about our work. Many of us don't want to be in our current work situation, but we feel stuck and can't get out of it, just as I was stuck in the car. For others, we feel we just have to do the job because we need the money to pay the bills. But we hate the job and we resent the amount of time it takes up. It doesn't fulfil us in any way. It just enables us to live to a standard that we like. For still others, it doesn't even do that. We just don't have any other choices. It's the only job we can get. But most commonly, we just can't seem to get the big picture on our work. The windscreen wipers have fallen off and we're completely lacking in vision – both our own vision and God's vision for us at work. I've lost count of the number of people who have said to me, 'I can't see how I'm making any difference at all for God in my work.'

So many Christians are lacking a vision for their work, and with that being the case, it's no wonder that there are so many Christians who aren't flourishing in their faith while at work. Just like me attempting to drive with my head stuck out of the window, we're not really sure how to cope with being a

Christian at work. We don't know what God wants from us when we're at work, but we're pretty sure we're not giving it to him, whatever it is that he's after.

If that's you, my hope and prayer is that by seeing your role as a trumpet at work, you will be helped, as it were, to put the windscreen wipers back on the car and enable yourself to have a clear vision of what you are about as a Christian in the workplace.

- You need to see your work as a trumpet fanfare – bringing glory to God.
- You need to see your work as a trumpet melody – a place where you are prepared to restrict your freedom by always looking to work so that other people don't stumble spiritually.
- You need to see your work as a trumpet call – a chance to urge your colleagues to wake up spiritually and come to Christ.

Even if you do forget the example of the trumpet (I hope you don't, but even if you do), then far more importantly, make sure you never forget the example of our chief trumpet player – the Lord Jesus Christ.

In the final sentence of the short paragraph that we have been focusing on in this chapter, Paul writes, 'Follow my example, as I follow the example of Christ' (1 Corinthians 11:1). To flourish for Christ at work, above all we should think, 'WWJD – What Would Jesus Do?'

When we think about the example of Christ, we know that his trumpet fanfare was to bring glory to God. We know that his trumpet melody was to use his amazing freedom, the freedom of being the second person of the Trinity, to restrict his freedom and become a man and take the very nature of a servant, and humble himself, and become obedient to death, even death on a cross. And we know that he did this because of his trumpet call – so that some might be saved.

In our workplaces we need to follow that example.

Recap

10. Glorifying God at work

Work is a trumpet fanfare
You are declaring the existence of someone important

Work is a trumpet melody
1. Work so non-Christians don't stumble
2. Work so Christians don't stumble
3. Work so everybody is pleased

Work is a trumpet call
You are a spiritual wake-up call to your colleagues

Relate

Name: Alex Webb-Peploe
Occupation: Illustrator

I love my job. I'm an illustrator/animator for a web agency and since I doodled throughout school (when I should have been paying attention), it's an absolute joy that someone is now prepared to pay me to draw. But please don't misunderstand me; there are days when work's a grind, when it's dull, and when my first instinct is to snap back at the pushy project manager or the critical client. It's the same for me as for most others I've spoken to.

However, my walk with Christ has completely transformed my understanding of work and the workplace and, as a result, my reactions to daily occurrences and battles are changing.

The gospel has been a powerful shaper of my attitude to the work itself. As I grow as a Christian, I'm learning that the day-to-day work I'm assigned needs to be done 'to the glory of God' – even when the boss isn't standing at my desk! The Lord created me to work and he's profoundly interested in my attitude to both my work and those alongside whom I work. My witness is displayed in both my work *and* my words.

When I first truly got to grips with what the gospel of Jesus Christ is, and how everyone needs to hear it, I was a bit overzealous in my evangelism. My workplace was my mission field and my colleagues were 'targets' for my apologetics and arguments.

Needless to say, my monologues didn't go down so well and while people generally thought I was an 'OK' guy (if a little weird), they were careful not to be caught alone in a room with me, just in case I launched into another 'sermon'.

I had been treating my colleagues like 'projects'. Each conversation required some reference to church, Christianity or Christ (or all of the above). If I had managed that, then it would have been a good chat. It didn't really matter where *they* were coming from . . .

What I needed to learn was that people don't care what you know until they know that you care. I needed to be interested in *them*. I needed to share life with them, and that meant time and energy. It meant going to the pub, hanging out at weekends and looking for opportunities to love and serve them.

So now, that's what I pray for. Opportunities to share life, to be a blessing in the workplace, as well as telling people the greatest news they'll ever hear. The great thing is that God is graciously restoring some of the friendships that were compromised by my earlier efforts.

As fallen human beings, all of us battle with frustration and pain in our lives, and gradually there are more opportunities to talk to and pray with my workmates as we get past the 'surface chit-chat' and share deeper issues.

I'm Jesus' only ambassador in my workplace . . . for the moment! My prayer is that he is glorified in that place.

Respond

1. Are there any ways in which you are causing other people at work to stumble spiritually by the way you are living?

2. How can you be 'all things to all people' at work so that 'by all possible means' you 'might save some'?

3. If you work in, or are about to work in, a regular workplace, then you are a front-line missionary for God. How does that make you feel?

11. SERVING GOD AT WORK

In his fantastic book *Don't Waste Your Life*, the American pastor John Piper comments, 'Thinking our work will glorify God when people do not know we are Christians is like admiring an effective ad on TV that never mentions the product. People may be impressed but they won't know what to buy.'[1]

The previous chapter was all about glorifying God at work, and it had a focus on our witness in the workplace as a trumpet calling people to Jesus. But working for the glory of God is, of course, far more than just evangelism. It's about our whole lives, and the next two chapters look at two other key aspects of glorifying God – serving God and worshipping God. If our faith is going to continue to flourish throughout our working lives, we need to be grounded on these realities. The honest truth is that the workplace is a tough mission field, and there will be many months and years when we will be frustrated if we are only thinking about our workplace as an opportunity for evangelism.

What do you think about your work?

My wife's parents live in Australia and a few years ago, when we were over there, I remember an advert on a huge billboard in the centre of Melbourne that caught my attention. The poster was divided in half. On the left-hand side was a blurred picture of workers walking fast across a road, in a hurry on their daily commute. On the right-hand side was a picture of a beautiful emerald-blue lake, with rugged hills in the background, the sun shining, and a couple sitting in a rowing boat on the lake. A picture of bliss. Every single person in the world would want to be in the right-hand picture rather than the left.

At the bottom of the left-hand side of the poster, under the picture of the commuters, was written 'Work-mania'. On the right-hand side of the poster, under the picture of the good-looking couple in the idyllic setting, was written . . . Can you guess?

'Tas-mania.'

It struck me as good advertising by the Tasmanian tourist board, because it was tapping into exactly what most of us think. Work is manic. It's a drag. It's certainly not peaceful and idyllic. Rather, it's full of stress. It's something we'd rather avoid. We find it frustrating.

Of course, there are some whose whole life revolves around their work. It takes up all their time, it takes up all their thoughts, it influences all their decisions. Take the film star Matt Damon. After one of his blockbusters as Jason Bourne, the interviewer asked him, 'How did you deal with all the craziness that comes with fame?'

Damon replied, 'It really was heady. It was such a huge thing to adjust to and the ripple effect of that really took time. It took time to get back to a place of inner calm. I felt out of balance for a while.'

So the interviewer pressed further, 'And how did you find that inner calm?'

'I hid in my work,' Damon admitted.

It's an honest answer, isn't it? I bet we all know people who are like that – hiding in their work.

Yet Matt Damon isn't just hiding in his work. The interviewer's next question was, 'What's your philosophy on life?'

Damon replied, 'To keep enjoying my work.' He's asked about his philosophy on life, but all he can focus on is his work. Work is his life.[2]

In general, in the world, there are two main views on work. Some people, like Matt Damon, see work as the ultimate source of fulfilment. They live to work and they live for work. Work is what drives them. Most of us, however, see work as something we'd prefer to avoid. For many of us, work is not the ultimate source of fulfilment, but the ultimate source of frustration.

What does God think about your work?

So that's us, but what about God? What does he think about work? One of the best bits of the Bible for answering this question is Paul's letter to the Colossians. In Colossae, there were some false teachers who were saying that God was interested in certain 'spiritual things' such as religious observance and spiritual experiences, but he wasn't interested in the everyday things of life. They were making a sacred-secular divide – saying that some areas of life were more important than others.

Now, before we start to judge them for this, let's look at ourselves. To what extent are we guilty of doing the same thing? Do you think God is more interested in share prices, refuse collection, computer systems and hat-making, or do you think that he is more interested in church services, Bible studies, Christianity Explored courses and Alpha courses?

Just like the false teachers in Colossae, we can very easily slip into thinking of some areas of life as being 'sacred' and therefore important to God, while we think of what we do in our workplaces as just being 'secular' and therefore of little importance to God. We so easily forget the reality that God is interested in all areas of our lives and that there is no such thing as a sacred-secular divide.

That's why we need to make sure we take to heart Paul's message in Colossians. From Colossians 3:1 onwards,

Paul spells out what it looks like to have Jesus as Lord in all areas of our lives: in our personal life (3:1–11), in our relationships with other Christians (3:12–17), in our family relationships (3:18–21), in our work relationships (3:22 – 4:1) and in our relationships with people who aren't yet Christians (4:2–6).

Paul is determined to counteract these false teachers in Colossae. Through this systematic description of all areas of life, he shows how God isn't just interested in the religious feasts, fasting and visions going on in Colossae. He's interested in all of life.

It's the same for us. God is interested in all areas of our lives and not just the seemingly 'spiritual' bits. Colossians 3:17 perhaps sums it up best: 'And whatever you do, whether in word or deed, do it all in the name of the Lord Jesus, giving thanks to God the Father through him.' Whatever we do, God is interested.

At the lunchtime services I used to run for workers in the West End of London, I often reminded people of this truth. I encouraged them to remember that God was just as interested in what they had been doing in their workplaces that morning as he was in the lunchtime service they were now attending. I repeated it again and again – because we humans so easily forget it.

A few years ago I met someone who, like me, was a management consultant, but was about to quit her job to go and work for a big evangelical church, where she was to be involved in a ministry to people in the workplace. I was really pleased for her and e-mailed her a couple of months later to see how she was doing. This is one sentence of her reply: 'Three weeks in and so far working for God is fab!'

Did you spot the problem with what she wrote? She thought that what she was doing working for the church was 'working for God', and so, by implication, what she was doing when she worked as a management consultant was not working for God. She was inadvertently displaying this false divide between the sacred and the secular.

It is indeed a false divide. It's also a dangerous divide. In my observation, it leads people at work in two directions.

Some people begin to suffer from 'second-rate Christian' syndrome, when they start believing that because they aren't working for a Christian organization, they are somehow inferior as Christians. I've met plenty of people like this – and if that's you, you need to be encouraged that you can serve God just as effectively in the workplace as anywhere else. It was Bishop J. C. Ryle who wrote, 'God may be glorified as really and truly in the secular calling as in the pulpit. Converted men (or women) can be eminently useful as land-lords, magistrates, soldiers, sailors, barristers or merchants. We want witnesses for Christ in all these professions.'[3] How right he is.

Other people end up suffering from 'double-life Christian' syndrome. This is when they behave one way in the church environment and another way in the workplace. Someone like this needs to hear, not so much encouragement, but challenge. Christ's call on our life is a total call – in all areas, including our workplace. I'm sure there are many Christians who are thought to be very self-controlled and calm at church, but who are known to have a sharp temper at work. Here are a couple of good questions to ask yourself to assess whether you suffer from 'double-life Christian' syndrome. If a member of your family or your church were to be a fly on the wall at your workplace, would they be surprised by what they observed of you? And if some of your work colleagues observed what you got up to and how you lived at the weekends, would they be flabbergasted at the contrast?

How does God want us to work?

> Slaves, obey your earthly masters in everything; and do it,
> not only when their eye is on you and to win their favour, but
> with sincerity of heart and reverence for the Lord. Whatever
> you do, work at it with all your heart, as working for the
> Lord, not for men, since you know that you will receive an
> inheritance from the Lord as a reward. It is the Lord Christ
> you are serving. Anyone who does wrong will be repaid for
> his wrong, and there is no favouritism.
> Masters, provide your slaves with what is right and fair,
> because you know that you also have a Master in heaven.
> (Colossians 3:22 – 4:1)

Your job may be a nightmare, but I doubt it is as tough as it
was being a slave in AD 60. We talk about being a slave to our
boss, or a slave to our company. You hear people calling their
bosses 'slave-drivers'. But the fact is, we can quit our jobs.
Slaves couldn't. All our jobs are a whole lot easier than being
a slave, and yet when we read how Paul tells slaves to live in
these verses in Colossians, it seems a huge task.

God wants us to obey our bosses, and not just if our boss
is good and kind. Even when the boss is being totally unreasonable, and demanding that we work really late into the night,
or that we work five night shifts on the trot, the consistent
teaching of the Bible seems to be that we should submit to
our boss. Obedience to the boss should be our attitude not
only when they are watching us, but all the time – even when
they are on holiday. In whatever we do, we're to give the task
our full attention, whether it's a high-powered meeting with
the chairman of the company, or cleaning or photocopying.

It's worth saying that the Bible does seem to give a couple
of exceptions as to when it's right *not* to obey our boss. One

is when the boss asks us to do something that goes clearly against what God would want (e.g. being asked to lie). In that situation, we can take our direction from Peter in Acts 5:29 when he says, 'We must obey God rather than men.' The other situation is when the boss is doing something which is not just unfair to you, but to someone else you work with. In that situation, for the sake of your colleague, you should speak up. So in Romans 12:18, Paul says, 'If it is possible, as far as it depends on you, live at peace with everyone,' but there will be times when your boss's actions are not just affecting you, and for that reason it is right to stand up against your boss. Despite these two exceptions, the general rule of thumb is that we obey our bosses in everything. Right actions in all things (v. 22a). Right motives at all times (v. 22b). Right efforts in all tasks (v. 23). It seems a ridiculously tall order, doesn't it? So why bother?

Why bother?

These verses in Colossians 3 give us two very powerful reasons as to why we should obey our boss. The first reason is that our *ultimate Boss* – the one we are really serving – is none other than the Lord Jesus Christ. Four times in five verses we read that we are serving and working for the Lord Jesus.

Seeing that Jesus is our ultimate Boss gives us a greater motivation to work in the way God wants us to. But it also gives us a new dignity. No longer are we just bowing down to our boss's power – we are doing things out of reverence for Christ. In *Thank God It's Monday* Mark Greene writes, 'When your boss asks you to do something, do you see Christ standing behind him/her saying "do it for me"?'[4] If we're able to get into the mindset of doing things for Christ, then we will be more prepared to do the mundane parts of our job well and in good cheer, because we're no longer just about people-pleasing, but about Christ-pleasing.

The second reason for working with right actions, motives and efforts is not so much the Boss, but the *incentive scheme*. Different organizations have different incentive schemes to try to get their employees working hard and to keep them loyal. The problem is that most of these incentive schemes don't offer very much incentive – perhaps the award of a pair of tartan slippers with a fluffy lamb's-wool inner lining for twenty years of loyal service. Or the promised reward fails to materialize. When I was a management consultant we had a scheme where we were given shares in the company. At one time I was told I'd get shares to the value of around £100,000. My shares are actually now worth around £6,000. Better than a kick in the teeth, but still a little disappointing.

However, the incentive scheme for the Christian is somewhat different. Paul says we will 'receive an inheritance from the Lord as a reward'. What is this inheritance? Well, earlier in the letter Paul states that the inheritance is all about our tasting what it is like in the kingdom of light where Jesus is King (Colossians 1:12). All Christians experience this in part now, but we will experience it fully, in all its complete and utter glory, in heaven for all eternity. There is no incentive scheme with a bigger reward – a perfect eternity with Christ.

There is also no other incentive scheme like this one where the reward is not performance related. So much in the workplace today is about our performance, but we don't qualify for this incentive scheme by how well we perform at serving Jesus in our work. Rather, God qualifies us. It's like no other incentive scheme. Colossians 1:12 says that God 'has qualified you to share in the inheritance of the saints in the kingdom of light' (Colossians 1:12). He did it. Not us. And he did it through the death of his Son.

What will happen when we serve Jesus at work?

When we look to work with right actions in all things, right motives at all times and right efforts in all tasks, we can't be certain of what will happen. Sometimes it will be positive. Perhaps we will be promoted early on because we are seen to be so reliable and hard-working. Perhaps people will notice the difference in us that Jesus makes, and they will be intrigued and want to ask us questions about our faith.

But sometimes what will happen may not feel so positive. Chang was a lawyer. He had a very good yearly appraisal from his boss with loads of positives, but then the appraisal finished with his boss saying to him that there was one problem in his work. 'If anything,' his boss said, 'you're a bit too Christian.'

Sometimes it's far more extreme than an isolated negative comment. Bill worked in a marketing firm and used to come to the breakfast Bible study I ran in London at the time. Then he got sacked from his job. Why? The two reasons Bill was given by his boss were that he had refused to lie on the telephone, and also, over the course of coffee breaks and lunches, he had spoken to some of his colleagues about the claims of Jesus. Bill was sacked because he refused to leave his Christian faith outside the door of his job.

Serving Jesus at work can have a negative impact on us. So we will only keep doing it if we remember that he is our ultimate Boss, and if we keep a clear focus on our amazing incentive scheme. It's only when we know that we will have it all in the future that we will be prepared to face hardship now.

Bill was prepared to face the termination of his job because he knew that he was part of a far better incentive scheme than his company could offer.

Bill served Jesus at work. He was a great trumpet player.

Recap

11. Serving God at work

What do **you** think about your work?		Fulfilling/frustrating
What does **God** think about your work?		He is interested in it
How does God want us to work?		**Obey the boss** • Right actions in all things • Right motives at all times • Right efforts in all tasks
Why bother?		• Our ultimate Boss • Our incentive scheme

Relate

Name: Lizzie Waterworth
Occupation: Voice-over artist

Up until fairly recently I had considered my job to be separate from my 'Christian' life. I believed that God was far more interested in my prayer life, my reading the Bible and going to church on Sundays, than what happens between 9 and 5 at the office – or, in my case, the studios in Soho, London.

I have been a freelance television voice-over artist for five years – voicing many familiar cartoon characters on television today. I am very fortunate in that I love my job and through it am constantly meeting new people – almost on a daily basis.

I remember a Christian friend once asking me how

difficult I found evangelizing in the workplace. I explained that I felt I was not really called to evangelize because I only met people for short periods of time – sometimes only a couple of hours. I went on to say that I didn't see how I could share the gospel in a few hours when I was supposed to be working, and how could I 'stand out' for him in such a short time, knowing I would probably never see these colleagues again? This was, of course, an excuse, but I was expecting my friend to nod and agree and was shocked when she replied with some words that I have never forgotten. She simply said, 'Have you considered that God has placed you in this unusual job and given you this gift of the ability to do different voices and accents so that you can represent God in Soho? You may be the only Christian your colleagues come across.' I felt incredibly ashamed, and it really hit me for the first time that it's no accident that I'm in the job I'm in. God has blessed me with so much, and I have a responsibility to be a good witness for him.

Every time I go to work I need to pray for strength to stand out, not to swear (despite being surrounded by swearing), not to laugh at certain jokes, not to drink too much with colleagues, and not to waste any opportunities that come up with regards to talking about him – even when I'm with colleagues for just a couple of hours. These may seem like small things in themselves, but I was encouraged recently when a famous singer I was working with made a comment about how I conducted myself in the studio, saying I was reliable and hard working. It would be easy for me to take the credit for this – but it gave me an opportunity to say that the only reason why I was like this was because of Jesus, and I gently brought him into the conversation.

It can be extremely difficult choosing to serve God at work, and so often I fail miserably – but God has promised that he is with us wherever we work, even in a dark downstairs studio in Soho!

Respond

1. How does it make you feel to know that God is interested in the work you are going to do?
2. Are there any ways in which you suffer from 'second-rate Christian' syndrome or 'double-life Christian' syndrome?
3. How does it change your view of work to know that your ultimate Boss at work is Jesus?

12. WORSHIPPING GOD AT WORK

Spot the odd one out:

1. Gin and tonic
2. Ant and Dec
3. Brussel sprouts and ice cream
4. Hammer and nail

I hope the answer is pretty obvious to you – because if you think that Brussel sprouts and ice cream make a good combination, then you are in need of greater help than this book can offer.

The slightly more serious question is whether 'work and worship' are like 'Brussel sprouts and ice cream'. Are work and worship two things that really can't and shouldn't go together?

One is all about long hours on a building site or in an office, shop or school. Early starts. Difficult customers. Unreasonable deadlines. Meetings. Stress. Sweat and toil. Coffee machines. Jumped-up urchins trying to tell us what to do. We all know about work. The other is all about singing. Church. Praise. Rainbow-strapped guitars. God. Music. People lifting their hands in adoration.

Work seems a million miles away from worship, doesn't it? And yet the same Hebrew word, *avodah*, can be translated as both worship and work.[1] It's surprising, isn't it? But it's true. So when you go into your workplace, that workplace is actually your worship-place. Work and worship are not like Brussel sprouts and ice cream. They go intimately together. And unless we realize this, we will never flourish for Christ in our workplaces.

A is for Act – the act of worship

> Therefore, I urge you, brothers, in view of God's mercy, to
> offer your bodies as living sacrifices, holy and pleasing to God
> – this is your spiritual act of worship.
> (Romans 12:1)

On first inspection, 'living' and 'sacrifice' are even less of a
pair than 'Brussel sprouts' and 'ice cream'. After all, the whole
point of a sacrifice is that it's killed. People would bring a
sheep, a goat or a bird to the temple and it would be killed.
Yet Paul talks here about our bodies being living sacrifices.
Our act of worship is no longer to bring a sacrifice, but to be
one ourselves. And we remain living.

It is all of us that is being offered. Worship is about what
I say with my tongue. It's about what I watch with my eyes.
It's about what I think with my mind. It's about how I use
my talents and gifts. It's about where I go with my feet. We
offer all of ourselves to God, at work as well as outside work.

We have not begun the act of worship when we feel nice
fuzzy feelings as we sing a worship song in church. We have
begun the act of worship only when we are offering our whole
lives to God. When we can say, 'Here I am, God. My whole
life is an offering to you. My relationships. My talents. My
time. My job. Please use every part of my life for your glory.'

Have you begun that act of worship? If you have, then
your work will be very much connected to your worship.

B is for Basis – the basis for worship

Romans is the biggest, longest and meatiest of all Paul's letters
in the New Testament. He says a lot and covers much ground
in the first eleven chapters, but he is still able to summarize
all that in just two words: *God's mercy*.

You haven't understood Christianity if you haven't realized that it is all about these two words: God's mercy. That's Christianity in a nutshell – God not giving us what we deserve.

Each one of us has not given God what he is due. We have withheld from him the praise, the love and the obedience that he deserves. He could demand the rightful punishment we deserve, but instead he does something very remarkable. Instead he offers us the gift of forgiveness, his Spirit, and eternal life. This gift cost God the death of his only Son, taking the punishment that we should have faced. God's mercy is God not giving us what we deserve, and also lavishing an amazing gift on us. If we have truly grasped God's mercy, we will be changed and want to change. God's mercy is the whole basis for wanting to offer our bodies as living sacrifices to God.

C is for Choice – the choice to worship

> Do not conform any longer to the pattern of this world, but
> be transformed by the renewing of your mind. Then you
> will be able to test and approve what God's will is – his good,
> pleasing and perfect will.
> (Romans 12:2)

The gospel of God's mercy is the basis for our worship at work, just as in the rest of life. As we become more amazed at the gospel, so we will have a greater desire to worship God at work. Yet there is an ongoing choice. Do we conform to the pattern of this world, or will we be transformed by the renewing of our minds?

It's very easy to sing 'I will offer up my life in spirit and truth, pouring out the oil of love as my worship to you'[2] in church on a Sunday. It is far more difficult to carry it out on a Monday when we are wrestling with a difficult colleague, a difficult customer or a difficult photocopier. Each day we are faced with the choice to worship God at work – by how we live, speak and act. But each day there is that temptation to conform to the pattern of our workplaces. We need God to be at work in us by the power of his Spirit to transform our minds, so that we can make decisions which are in line with God's will for us at work.

I once read of a church which had a sign that many churches have, which says, 'You are now entering a place of worship.' Except they didn't have it where most churches have the sign – on the way into the church. Instead they placed this sign above the main door, but on the inside, so that you saw the sign as you were heading out of the church building. That's a great visual illustration. Whatever we do each day and wherever we are each day is a place for us to worship. It's no wonder that Vaughan Roberts states, 'You cannot judge a church's worship by what happens in the hour or so when they meet on a Sunday. The real test is how its members behave during the rest of the week.'[3]

Workplace worship

> They devoted themselves to the apostles' teaching and to the fellowship, to the breaking of bread and to prayer . . . And the Lord added to their number daily those who were being saved. (Acts 2:42, 47)

At the end of Acts 2, we are given a glimpse of the four main aspects of the early Christian disciples in worship. Their worship is Bible-centred (the apostles' teaching), it's loving (the fellowship), it's dependent (the breaking of bread and prayer), and then, after some illustrations of how these are worked out, in verse 47 we see that their worship is also outward-looking (people being saved).

It's a great model for church worship, but it could just as well be a model of our workplace worship too.

Bible-centred workplace worship

This certainly does not mean bashing all our colleagues over the head with a Bible. But Bible-centred workplace worship does result in at least two things.

First, it enables us to *think Christianly about the job we do*. In his *Institutes of Christian Religion*, John Calvin says that the Bible is like a pair of glasses. If someone is shortsighted and they don't wear their glasses, then everything is blurred. Their glasses help them to see clearly what, unaided, they can't see clearly. It's the same with the Bible. Without it, we only have a blurred understanding of this world. We need to view the world through the lens of the Bible to give us clarity, insight and understanding – and that includes everything that goes on in our work. If our workplace worship is going to please God, we will need to look out on our work through the lens of the Bible. Otherwise we'll find ourselves going blurrily through our working life, making the wrong decisions, bumping into things and causing havoc – just like a short-sighted person without their glasses.

As much as we might like to share the gospel with all our colleagues in the first month of work, that is unlikely to happen. Of course we should pray for opportunities and take opportunities, but the reality is that we are not being paid to evangelize. We are, however, being paid to do our job – and so we need to think Christianly about the job we do by looking at it through the lens of the Bible.

Let me give you three examples of this from people I met during my time at All Souls. Geoff works as a news correspondent for a main media broadcasting organization. When I spoke to him, he said one of his central aims in work is to ensure that the truth is always communicated in all the reports he is involved in. Not surprisingly, he can't get the organization to report regularly on why Jesus is Lord on their TV news programmes, but Geoff can always ensure that his reports carry the hallmark of the God of all truth.

Mo used to work as a storyliner and is now a script editor for one of the well-known soap operas on TV. Again, she is not going to be able to have regular storylines involving people hearing the good news of the gospel and getting saved. After all, generally when a character is a 'Christian' on one of these programmes, they're usually portrayed as being two pence short of a lamb chop. But as Mo has viewed her work through the lens of the Bible, she aims consistently to promote story-lines which remind people that their actions always have consequences.

John is a professor of neo-natal medicine at a London hospital. In his work with premature babies, he has seen how one of his roles is to speak up for the right of children in the womb to live, in the face of the abortion laws. It's not an easy role, and John has faced a lot of adverse pressure for his stance, but he has thought Christianly about his job, and acted in light of that.

Now, we may not be a news correspondent, or a script-writer, or a medical professor, but in whatever job we do, we can still think Christianly about it as we view it through the lens of the Bible.

Bible-centred workplace worship also allows us to do a second thing. It enables us *to live Christianly in the job we do*.

I remember many years ago when I went interrailing with a couple of mates. We were in Florence and we had just had a big argument about whether it would be better to buy warm beer or warm wine to drink (as you do). Two of us thought wine, and one guy, Ian, thought beer. So the two out-voted the one, we bought the wine, and there we were walking down the street with Ian in a sulk behind us because he hadn't got his warm beer. And then, just to increase the injustice of it all, a pigeon decided it would be fun to use Ian for target practice, and he was hit by the most enormous slimy pigeon poo.

Now what did Ian do? He went to the nearest shop window to look at his reflection, saw where the pigeon poo was, saw he was a mess, then took his T-shirt off and washed it and his hair in one of the fountains in Florence. He looked in the window and did something about the mess that he saw.

Yet what do we often do with the Bible? Well, it's the equivalent of being hit by the pigeon poo: we look in the shop window to see that it's definitely there, it's really bad, it's really noticeable, we're an absolute mess. But then we walk on and do nothing about it. That's what James writes in his letter in the New Testament, anyway: 'Anyone who listens to the word but does not do what it says is like a man who looks at his face in a mirror and, after looking at himself, goes away and immediately forgets what he looks like' (James 1:23–24). The Bible hits us, it challenges us, it acts like a mirror on our lives, showing where we're in a mess. It shows us our spiritual state, and yet we do nothing about it. At least, if you're any-thing like me a lot of the time, you do nothing about it.

As we go through our working lives, of course we need to be reading the Bible daily. But it's no good just reading it. We actually need to respond to what it says. When what we read challenges how we relate to our boss, when it challenges how we gossip, when it challenges how we fill in our time sheet – whatever it is, we need to *do* what it says.

I still remember a searching question that challenged me when I heard it in a sermon as a student – and which still challenges me now every time I think of it. The question is this: 'Can you name one thing that you have changed in your life in the last month as a result of what you have read in the Bible?'

Just one thing.

Well, can you?

I confess that for me there are many months when I can't name a single thing. And that's not good.

Loving workplace worship

This chapter began with reference to Romans 12:1–2. This is what the theologian David Peterson has written about these verses: 'The first two verses of Romans 12 place the concluding chapters of the letter under the umbrella of worship.'[4] When we read chapters 12 – 16 of the letter, we see that this worship is all about transformed relationships. It may seem surprising that worship is about transformed relationships, but if you think about it, it makes sense. I don't know about you, but it's my relationships which most need transforming. It's in my relationships where most of my sin is carried out. Take the workplace. If you ask almost anybody what they complain most about connected to their work, the answer will almost always be some of the people they work with. We find it very difficult to have loving working relationships.

That's why workplace worship that is pleasing to God is focused on the need to be loving. When you read the last chapters of Romans, they include comments on relating to different sorts of colleagues, including those we find difficult (Romans 12:17–18), those who are in authority over us (Romans 13:7) and those who work next to us (Romans 13:10). But all of them centre on the need to show love to our different colleagues.

What will loving workplace worship look like? The list is endless. A birthday cake. A cup of tea. An offer of help. An offer of support. It's nothing extraordinary – just showing practical love to people, little acts of kindness, even to people who don't like us, taking our lead from our Lord.

Dependent workplace worship

You would think it would be a real joy and delight that as Christians we can pray about things at work and depend on the Lord. Yet my experience, and the experience of most people I talk to, is that because the culture of the workplace seems to be all about being self-sufficient and showing how impressive, capable and competent we are, it's very easy to fall into the same thinking and end up depending on ourselves rather than on God.

In his pamphlet on practising God's presence at work, David Prior writes, 'All would agree, in principle, to the truth that God is present with them in their work . . . From time to time, perhaps during a crisis or a rare slack period, they make the opportunity to practise God's presence – to pray about their work, their colleagues, their pressures. But it is rare.'[5]

There are practical things we can do to encourage our workplace worship to be dependent. Some people, as they walk into their place of work each morning, consciously say, 'Good morning, Lord,' to remind themselves that God is already there welcoming them. Others put a Bible verse on their computer screensaver or stick one on their phone.

However, I actually think the greatest help to depending on God at work is simply to remind ourselves who God is. Take the bit of the Sermon on the Mount that we didn't look at in Part 3 – the Lord's Prayer. How does Jesus start that prayer? 'Our Father in Heaven.' That is who God is.

If God was just our Father, but not in heaven, he wouldn't have the power to intervene in our lives for our good and we wouldn't bother depending on him. But it's the same the other way round too. If God was just in heaven, but he wasn't our Father, then he might be powerful, but there'd be no guarantee that we would have from God what is best for us as individuals. Again, we wouldn't bother depending on him. When we remember that he is 'Our Father' and 'in heaven', then we will be motivated to depend on him.

Outward-looking workplace worship

C. S. Lewis was not just the author of the *Narnia Chronicles*. He taught as a fellow of Magdalen College, Oxford for nearly thirty years, and later was a fellow of Magdalene College, Cambridge and the first professor of Medieval and Renaissance literature. This was what he, as a literature professor, wrote:

> The Christian will take literature a little less seriously than the cultured Pagan . . . The unbeliever is always apt to make a kind of religion of his aesthetic experiences . . . But the Christian knows from the outset that the salvation of a single soul is more important than the production or preservation of all the epics and tragedies in the world.[6]

Having this right perspective did not mean that C. S. Lewis stopped being a literature professor to become an itinerant evangelist, but it did mean he realized that a hugely significant part of his workplace worship was outward-looking. In his work, he looked to have meaningful relationships with those he came into contact with, as a vehicle for telling them the good news of the gospel.

That must be our aim too. We should see ourselves as signposts to Jesus in our workplaces.[7] To do that, we must live lives at work that honour Jesus, but we must also have lips that actually speak of Jesus. Life and lip must go together. If we aren't actually speaking of Jesus, then we won't be pointing to him at all. That means moving on from conversations where we tell colleagues that we went to church, to conversations which are about the truth of the gospel. That's not easy, but if we want to display outward-looking workplace worship, that's the challenge we face.

The truth is, there is one difference between worshipping God at work and playing the trumpet. Playing the trumpet is hindered if our mouth is too big. Worshipping God at work is hindered if our mouth is too small.

Recap

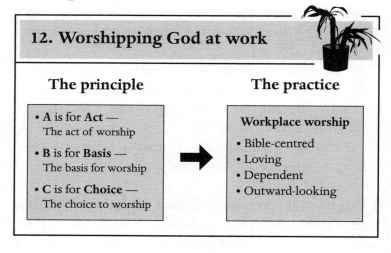

12. Worshipping God at work

The principle

- **A** is for **Act** —
  The act of worship
- **B** is for **Basis** —
  The basis for worship
- **C** is for **Choice** —
  The choice to worship

The practice

Workplace worship

- Bible-centred
- Loving
- Dependent
- Outward-looking

Relate

Name: Colin Paterson
Occupation: Entertainment reporter for BBC radio

There are many occupations which feature in the Bible. Jesus was a carpenter. Paul, Aquila and Priscilla made tents, Joseph ended up in jail with a butler, and in the Gospels there are more fishermen than you can shake a rod at.

Sadly, unless I'm very much mistaken, the Good Book contains not a single mention of an entertainment reporter.

I've tried to work out which biblical characters are closest to sharing my profession. Recently I had to cover the birth of Angelina Jolie's and Brad Pitt's twins. In the Bible, who is it who has the duty of reporting the most important births? The angels. Result.

OK, I admit, the comparison does not stand up. Indeed, far from it. Often my work can seem so fatuous and superficial that it can be hard to see how I could possibly worship God through it.

Unless you are in a job saving lives, bringing people to justice or helping to educate future generations, it can be incredibly difficult to equate what you are doing for a living with praising the Lord. There is a temptation to believe that your place of work is unfit for worship. Can a radio report on Amy Winehouse's latest visit to rehab really be equated with the singing of hymns in church? The rational answer would be, 'No, no, no.' In reality it is, 'Yes, yes, yes.'

No matter how mundane or superficial jobs may appear to be, God can use them. He places people in all kinds of occupations, in a huge variety of locations, for all sorts of different reasons. My side of the deal is to 'do everything for the glory of God' – and it is that 'everything' which is the tricky bit. I cannot compartmentalize my life. My time at work belongs to God and therefore I am to worship him there, not just call on him when I fancy a promotion or want an awkward colleague to be moved.

I've come to realize that worshipping God at work falls into two categories. First, there is the matter of using my skills to the best of my ability. God gave me these and loves seeing them in action.

Second, there is the worship of God at work through my witness. It's humbling and sobering to think that I can be in my current position because of one single person whom God is going to bring across my path. My 'worshipping of God' in the workplace might well be an essential part of God's plan for that person. I cringe as I write this, thinking of separate 'at work' incidents where a telephone and a metal bucket received treatment from me which was definitely not worship.

So as I stand on a red carpet with microphone in hand, I console myself with the knowledge that yes, God may not be that interested in who has won 'Best Soap Villain' at the TV Choice Awards, but for that night the most mundane celebrity bash in town is to be my place of worship.

Respond

1. Have you ever thought of your workplace as your 'worship place'? How does it make you feel?

2. Have you begun to think about how to do your work through the lens of the Bible? What might this mean for your work?

3. Could you say that you are a 'signpost to Jesus' at work?

CONCLUSION

WORK – VIEWED THROUGH A TARDIS

I hope that this book has been and will continue to be a help to you in working without wilting in your faith. My desire is that the four parts of the book – Treadmill, Trampoline, Trout and Trumpet – will all combine to motivate and give you resources to keep living for Christ and shining for him throughout your working life.

However, to wrap up this book, I'm going to suggest something that is perhaps unexpected. I'm convinced that the best way to bring together all the different elements of this book is to view work through a Tardis. Doctor Who, of course, brought 'the Tardis' into the world – the time-travel machine which looks like a 1950s-style London police box and is famously bigger on the inside than the outside. And so, like the Doctor, I'd like to invite you to do some time travel right now. Would you step into the Tardis – without the sound effects, I'm afraid – and come on a journey through time? First stop is all the way back to the creation of the world. What, if anything, can we learn about our work from Eden?

Work in Eden

Whatever your view on how literally to take Genesis 1 – 3, you can be certain that we are meant to understand from the first few chapters of the Bible that God created the world. It's clear that God is a worker himself – he worked to create the world. And it's clear that God made us to work too.

So in this perfect Garden of Eden setting, work existed. There was manual work: 'The LORD God took the man and put him in the Garden of Eden to work it and take care of it' (Genesis 2:15). And there was academic work: 'Now the LORD God had formed out of the ground all the beasts of the field and all the birds of the air. He brought them to the man to see what he would name them; and whatever the man called each living creature, that was its name' (Genesis 2:19). So we can see that all work, paid or not, is part of God's good creation, and that has huge implications.

Work is a source of satisfaction

There is nothing inherently bad about work; it is a source of satisfaction. Work was there before the fall and before sin entered humans. In fact, it's worth noticing that Eden wasn't a playground, but a place of work. It reminds us that work is not a punishment but a blessing. Work is a good thing. Work is not something we should try and escape. As much as we enjoy holidays, in our heart of hearts we all know that idleness can never be our ultimate goal. Humans have always been meant to work.

Work is not the ultimate source of satisfaction

By the seventh day God had finished the work he had been doing; so on the seventh day he rested from all his work. And God blessed the seventh day and made it holy,

because on it he rested from all the work of creating that
he had done.
(Genesis 2:2–3)

God resting doesn't mean that God sat back in his celestial
armchair and took a very long holiday. Rather, the reason
why God rested was that he had just created humans, the
pinnacle of his creation, and he had brought humans into
relationship with him. That fits with the rest of the Bible.
Jesus famously said, 'Come to me, all you who are weary
and burdened, and I will give you rest' (Matthew 11:28), and
he wasn't talking about sending us to rest and recuperate
on some luxury cruise. Rest in the Bible is not about rest on
holiday – it's about rest in your heart as you come into
relationship with the Lord Jesus Christ. It's the same in
the creation account. The Lord God rested from his
work when he had brought humans into the rest of being
in relationship with him. As St Augustine prayed, 'Lord –
our hearts are restless until they find their rest in you.'
That's what we were made for – to be in relationship with
God. That's where ultimate satisfaction is found, not in
our work.[1]

Work is a source of frustration
I guess this isn't a surprise to you, but in Genesis 3 we discover
why work can be frustrating. It's because of humans falling
out of relationship with God and being banished from Eden.
There was still the *command* to work – 'So the LORD God
banished him from the Garden of Eden to work the ground
from which he had been taken' (Genesis 3:23) – but outside
Eden, the *character* of work became very different. No longer
was it always fulfilling; it became frustrating as well. The
curses that God gave make this explicit:

Cursed is the ground because of you;
　　through painful toil you will eat of it
　　all the days of your life.
It will produce thorns and thistles for you,
　　and you will eat the plants of the field.
By the sweat of your brow
　　you will eat your food.
(Genesis 3:17–19)

The best way of summarizing what our time travel to Eden shows us about our work is to say that it shows us how work is like a stormy lover. We can't live with work, but we can't live without it either. I hope you've seen this tension throughout the book. Work frustrates us, but it fulfils us too. Like a lover, it brings satisfaction at times – but it can never ultimately satisfy.

Work in eternity

First stop in the Tardis was going back to Eden. The second stop is in the opposite direction – eternity. As we observe eternity, we also discover things which influence our view about our work.

Eternity is a place of perfect rest

Right now, even if we have a relationship with Jesus, we don't experience ultimate satisfaction. We don't know complete rest in all its fullness. We're not immune from frustrations, suffering and difficulties just because we trust in Christ. But that perfect rest will come for all Christians. Heaven will be a place of perfect rest.

Yet, does this mean that in heaven there will be no work at all? Will heaven be a giant pool party with angels floating around offering us divine cocktails while we lounge on our lilos?

Eternity is a place of perfect work

We tend to think that things like our work which happen here on earth are nothing more than temporary and transient. The Bible paints a different picture. When Jesus returns, God is not going to obliterate this earth, but he will renew it, redeem it and liberate it from its bondage to decay (Romans 8:18–22). The city is Revelation's picture of the new creation and this is how it is described:

> The city does not need the sun or the moon to shine on it, for the glory of God gives it light, and the Lamb is its lamp. The nations will walk by its light, and the kings of the earth will bring their splendour into it. On no day will its gates ever be shut, for there will be no night there. The glory and honour of the nations will be brought into it. Nothing impure will ever enter it, nor will anyone who does what is shameful or deceitful, but only those whose names are written in the Lamb's book of life. (Revelation 21:23–27)

We see that eternity has a very real, physical dimension to it. All those trusting in Jesus – those written in the Lamb's book of life – will be in this City. But that's not all. The 'splendour', the 'glory' and the 'honour' of kings and nations will be in the city, and that must include human work. This human work will be purified and redeemed, so that it is free from sin just as we will be free from sin. But work will certainly be a part of the new creation.[2]

Wonderfully, the curses of Genesis 3 will finally be removed: 'No longer will there be any curse. The throne of God and of the Lamb will be in the city, and his servants will serve him' (Revelation 22:3). But work will not be removed. Eternity will not be the giant pool party of 100% leisure and 0% work that we might have imagined. After all, an eternal pool party would get very boring after a bit – and we'd get very wrinkly skin. Eternity will involve work, the work of serving the Lord Jesus Christ. But this is perfect work. It is work which utterly fulfils and which in no way frustrates.

Work on earth

But so what? As our Tardis lands back in the twenty-first century, what difference does all that we've learned from our time travel make?

The value of work

So often we are tempted to think that God isn't too fussed about our work. Actually, our work has great value, even if we don't realize it. In our work, we are involved in something that God thinks is important and worthwhile.

- We are commanded by God to work.
- God says there is a satisfaction to be had in our work.
- We are serving the Lord in and through our work.
- Our work is not temporary and earthly, but has an eternal dimension to it.

That has got to transform our perspective on a Monday morning, whatever our work is. If you are about to step into the workplace for the first time, please don't think that your work is not of interest to God. He cares passionately about all aspects of what you are going to be doing.

The priority in work

There is one other thing that we have seen through our Tardis travel. People matter most to God. People are his top priority.

- People are the ones made in God's image.
- God rested only when he had made people and brought them into relationship with himself.
- Jesus came to earth primarily to bring people back into that perfect rest with God.
- People matter most to God – and so people should matter most to us too.

It is right to say, then, that there is a work that all Christians are involved in over and above the work of our job. We are working to encourage other people to have eternal rest. That has to be our top priority in work – it's more important than getting promoted; more important than being well-respected; more important than being fulfilled by our work.

Our top priority is to be working, living and speaking in such a way that we point other people to the one who provides us with that eternal rest.

The value of work. The priority in work. I believe that holding on to these two points – fully thought through, fully internalized – will be enough to ensure that, as you continue throughout your working life, you will not just work without wilting in your faith, but you will positively flourish for the Lord in your work, and bear much fruit.

Fruit in his name and for his glory.

NOTES

Chapter 1
1 'Why Dilbert is Right', *Gallup Management Journal*, 9 March 2006.

Chapter 3
1 Paul Valler, *Get a Life* (IVP, 2008), p. 29.

Part 2
1 Quoted in Anushka Asthana, 'They don't live to work . . . they work to live', *Observer on Sunday*, 25 May 2008.

Chapter 4
1 See The Work Foundation website, www.theworkfoundation.com.
2 Quoted on The Work Foundation website, www.theworkfoundation.com.
3 Sally O'Reilly, 'Life in Slow Motion', *Guardian*, 19 May 2008.
4 Mark Greene, *Supporting the Workers*.
5 Paul Valler, *Get a Life* (IVP, 2008).
6 Tim Chester, *The Busy Christian's Guide to Busyness* (IVP, 2006), p. 71.
7 *Evening Standard*, magazine supplement, 17 November 2006.
8 Chester, *The Busy Christian's Guide to Busyness*, p. 75.
9 See the discussion on the place of money in Tony Payne and Peter Jensen, *Guidance and the Voice of God* (Matthias Press, 1997), p. 129.
10 John Piper, *Don't Waste Your Life* (Crossway, 2003), p. 132.

Chapter 5

1 Rick Warren, *The Purpose Driven Life* (Zondervan, 2003).
2 Lisa Beamer, Betty Robison and Ken Abraham, *Let's Roll* (Tyndale House, 2002).

Part 3

1 John Stott, *The Message of the Sermon on the Mount*, The Bible Speaks Today commentary series, 2nd rev. ed. (IVP, 1993).
2 J. John, *Ten: Living the Ten Commandments in the 21st Century* (Kingsway, 2000).

Chapter 6

1 Thanks to Nathan Morgan Locke for these phrases.
2 Nicky Gumbel, *Questions of Life*, new ed. (Kingsway, 2001).
3 Nicky Gumbel, *Challenging Lifestyle*, new ed. (Kingsway, 1996), p. 34.

Chapter 7

1 Vault 2008 Office Romance Survey; see www.vault.com/office-romance.
2 Kate Hilpen in the *Guardian*, Monday 27 September 2004.
3 A worker in Bedford on the BBC website, http://news.bbc.co.uk/nolpda/ukfs_news/hi/newsid 3811000/3811937.stm

Chapter 8

1 Gerald Ratner, *The Rise and Fall . . . and Rise Again* (Capstone, 2007).
2 Ian Garrett, sermon on Matthew 6 – Treasure, 21 January 2003.
3 Ian Garrett, sermon on Matthew 6 – Wealth, 9 August 1998.
4 Stefan Stern, 'In the Market for a Messiah', *Financial Times*, 5 September 2007.

5 See Tim Vickers, *Transition* (UCCF, 2003), p. 36.

6 Ken Costa, *God at Work* (Continuum, 2007), p. 174.

7 Al Stewart, *The Briefing*, issue 349, p. 18.

8 Rico Tice and Barry Cooper, *Christianity Explored* (Authentic, 2002).

Chapter 9

1 http://news.bbc.co.uk/1/hi/health/763401.stm.

2 http://www.tssa.org.uk/article-47.php3?id_article=986.

3 http://www.jobsite.co.uk/career/advice/health.html.

4 http://findarticles.com/p/articles/mi_qn4158/is_19991010/ai_n14279567.

5 V. A. Worwood, *The Fragrant Mind* (Bantam Books, 1997).

6 John Stott, *The Message of the Sermon on the Mount*, The Bible Speaks Today commentary series, 2nd rev. ed. (IVP, 1993), p. 169.

7 Ibid., p. 165.

Chapter 10

1 Mark Greene, *Thank God It's Monday*, rev. ed. (Scripture Union, 1999) in chapter 1.

2 Operation World.

Chapter 11

1 John Piper, *Don't Waste Your Life* (Crossway, 2003), p. 143.

2 Interview in Australian magazine *NW*, 30 August 2004, p. 69.

3 J. C. Ryle – 'Expository Thoughts on Mark 5:18–20', http://www.sermonindex.net/modules/articles/article_pdf.php?aid=2087

4 Mark Greene, *Thank God It's Monday*, rev. ed. (Scripture Union, 1990), p. 119.

Chapter 12

1 Mark Greene, *Thank God It's Monday*, rev. ed. (Scripture Union, 2001), p. 24.

2 Lyrics by Matt Redman.

3 Vaughan Roberts, *True Worship* (Paternoster, 2002), p. 24. Read this excellent book (especially chapter 2) for more thinking on how Romans 12:1–2 speaks about a whole life of worship.

4 Quoted in Roberts, *True Worship*, p. 24, from David Peterson, *Engaging with God* (IVP, 1992), p. 178.

5 David Prior, *Practising God's Presence at Work*, Centre for Marketplace Theology Papers, No. 2.

6 C. S. Lewis, 'Christianity and Literature', in *Christian Reflections* (Eerdmans, 1996), p. 10.

7 This idea is borrowed and adapted from Tim Vickers.

Conclusion

1 I am grateful to Paul Williams for helping me to see this.

2 To think more on this idea, read Darrel Cosden, *The Heavenly Good of Earthly Work* (Paternoster, 2006).

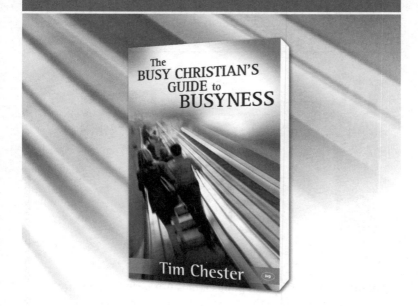